A Church Organized and Functioning

W. L. Howse and W. O. Thomason

Revised Edition

CONVENTION PRESS 2281

NASHVILLE   TENNESSEE

Code Number: Church Study Course
This book is number 0105 in category 1, section
for Adults and Young People
Library of Congress catalog card number: 66-20873
Printed in the United States of America
20. MH 68 R.R.D.

CONTENTS

ABOUT THE AUTHORS

W. L. HOWSE, *Director,* Education Division, Baptist Sunday School Board, Nashville, Tennessee

W. O. THOMASON, *Assistant to Director,* Education Division, Baptist Sunday School Board, Nashville, Tennessee

GEORGE W. SCHROEDER, *Executive Secretary,* Brotherhood Commission, Memphis, Tennessee, and commission staff

HOWARD B. FOSHEE, *Secretary,* Church Administration Department, Baptist Sunday School Board, and department staff

W. HINES SIMS, *Secretary,* Church Music Department, Baptist Sunday School Board, and department staff

A. V. WASHBURN, *Secretary,* Sunday School Department, Baptist Sunday School Board, and department staff

PHILIP B. HARRIS, *Secretary,* Training Union Department, Baptist Sunday School Board, and department staff

ALMA HUNT, *Executive Secretary,* Woman's Missionary Union, Birmingham, Alabama, and Promotion Division staff

CHURCH STUDY COURSE

THE CHURCH STUDY COURSE began October 1, 1959. It is a merger of three courses previously promoted by the Sunday School Board: the Sunday School Training Course, the Graded Training Union Study Course, and the Church Music Training Course. On October 1, 1961, the Woman's Missionary Union principles and methods studies were added. On January 1, 1967, the Brotherhood Commission principles and methods studies were added.

The course is fully graded. The system of awards provides a series of five diplomas of twenty books each for Adults or Young People, two diplomas of five books each for Intermediates, and two diplomas of five books each for Juniors.

The course is comprehensive, with books grouped into twenty-one categories. The purpose of the course is to help Christians to grow in knowledge and conviction, to help them to grow toward maturity in Christian character and competence for service, to encourage them to participate worthily as workers in their churches and to develop leaders for all phases of church life and work.

The Church Study Course is promoted by the Baptist Sunday School Board, 127 Ninth Avenue, North, Nashville, Tennessee 37203, through its Sunday School, Training Union, Church Music, and Church Administration departments; by the Woman's Missionary Union, 600 North Twentieth Street, Birmingham, Alabama 35203; by the Brotherhood Commission, 1548 Poplar Avenue, Memphis, Tennessee 38104; and by the respective departments in the states affiliated with the Southern Baptist Convention. A description of the course and the system of awards may be found in the leaflet "Trained Workmen," which may be obtained without charge from any one of these departments.

A record of all awards earned should be maintained in each church. A person should be designated by the church to keep the files. Forms for such records may be ordered from any Baptist Book Store.

REQUIREMENTS FOR CREDIT FOR CLASS OR HOME STUDY

IF CREDIT is desired for the study of this book in class or by the home study method, the following requirements must be met:

I. CLASS METHOD

1. The class must meet a minimum of six clock hours. The required time does not include assembly periods.

2. A class member who attends all class sessions and reads the book will not be required to do any written work.

3. A class member who is absent from one or more class sessions must read the book and answer the questions on all chapters he misses.

4. The teacher should request an award for himself. A person who teaches a book in sections for Intermediates or Juniors of any category or conducts an approved unit of instruction for Nursery, Beginner, or Primary children will be granted an award in category 11, Special Studies, which will count as an elective on his own diploma. He should specify in his request the name of the book taught or unit conducted for Nursery, Beginner, or Primary children.

Credit will be given to "team teachers" when they cooperatively plan the teaching procedures and attend and share responsibility in each teaching session.

5. The teacher should complete the "Request for Book Award" (Form 151) and forward it to the Church Study Course Awards Office, 127 Ninth Avenue, North, Nashville, Tennessee 37203.

II. INDIVIDUAL HOME STUDY

1. A person who does not attend any class session may receive credit by answering all questions for written work as indicated in the book or in a designated periodical. When a person turns in his paper on home study, he must certify that he has read the book.

2. Students may find profit in studying the text together, but individual papers are required. Carbon copies or duplicates in any form cannot be accepted.

3. Home study work papers may be graded by the pastor or a person designated by him, or they may be sent to the Church Study Course Awards Office for grading. The form entitled "Request for Book Award" (Form 151) must be used in requesting awards. It should be mailed to the Church Study Course Awards Office, 127 Ninth Avenue, North, Nashville, Tennessee 37203.

4. Credit for home study of mission study books not containing questions is earned by writing a synopsis of each chapter.

III. CREDIT FOR THIS BOOK

This book is number 0105 in category 1, section for Adults and Young People.

Introduction

IF THIS BOOK may be likened to a river, several streams of action as tributaries flow together to make it what it is.

In 1959, the Southern Baptist Convention, meeting in Louisville, Kentucky, adopted a recommendation of its committee on total program that one of the functions of the Executive Committee should be: "To maintain an official organization manual defining the responsibilities of each agency of the Convention for conducting specific programs and for performing other functions."

This action subsequently called for the Southern Baptist Convention agencies to define their programs and to budget and report on them each year.

In carrying out the instructions of the Convention, those responsible for designing the educational programs at the Sunday School Board found it imperative to make a new study of the church and its basic tasks.

Twelve persons in the Education Division of the Sunday School Board were asked to devote nine months of their time to stating and defining the functions of a church. This task force met daily for several weeks to study the nature and functions of New Testament churches. Then members of the task force went in teams of two to twenty-one selected churches to study with them the functions of New Testament churches. As a result of this study, the churches agreed that to worship, to proclaim, to educate, and to minister are basic functions of a church.

Another stream of action which became a tributary to this manuscript was the study of the program assignments of the Southern Baptist Convention to the Sunday School Board from 1845 to 1962. The Historical Commission of the Southern Baptist Convention researched the material upon which this study was made. Using this information, the Convention agencies responsible for developing suggested church educational programs analyzed their work to make certain that all Convention assignments were included in their programs.

Another tributary to this book has been the development of a long-range planning service by the Church Administration Department of the Sunday School Board. This department, acting for the denomination, has worked with all Convention agencies in developing materials for church long-range planning. The functions of a church formulated by the task force have been used as basic concepts in these materials. Valuable help has come from the pilot churches which have participated in long-range planning and from resource panels representative of all Convention agencies.

These concurrent developments have contributed to the concepts which are represented on the pages of this book. These developments, all of which seem providential, are rooted in the New Testament and the historical assignments of the Southern Baptist Convention. At least one thousand persons have seen much, if not all, of this material in various forms. Those responsible for contributing to it are representatives of Southern Baptist Convention agencies, state convention personnel, seminary professors, workers in the associations, pastors, church staff members, and volunteer workers in the churches.

The entire approach begins with the church as established by Christ and places it at the center of all planning and programing. It is in this context that the tasks of a church and its organizations have been stated so that a church may organize itself to function more effectively.

The statement of tasks in terms of the nature and functions of a church achieved correlation and provided the basis for the coordination of a church's programs. As Southern Baptist Convention agency personnel developed program suggestions and curriculum materials from this correlated base, they tested the validity of the statement and they also gained deeper insights into the concepts of correlation it expressed.

The first edition of the book was published in May, 1963. Since then approximately 100,000 copies have been circulated. The questions, comments, and suggestions from those who studied the book increased the understanding of the content covered.

All of these insights called for a new edition of *A Church Organized and Functioning* which would reflect the deeper understandings of the original concepts. This second edition probably expresses the greatest team effort by church program, program service, and administrative service leaders in the history of the Southern Baptist Convention.

This type of service to the churches was recognized by the Executive Committee of the Southern Baptist Convention in adopting the report of its Program Committee, February 25, 1965:

The Program Committee wishes to report that these three agencies (Baptist Sunday School Board, Woman's Missionary Union, and Brotherhood Commission) are to be commended in their search to find a way to solve the problem of correlation. They also are to be commended for their effort to advance the programs of their various agencies, providing maximum efficiency to assist the churches in their tasks of bringing men to God through Christ; and to do their planning on a long-range basis. We believe that it should be recognized that the work that goes into this planning by the men and women of these agencies must be endless and exhaustive. Surely the denomination is grateful.

CHAPTER 1

1

The Nature of a Church

EVIL FORCES abound in our world today. Confusion, hatred, and fear are created by these forces. Turmoil, hate, and rebellion in individual lives and in nations cause many people to lose hope for the future of our world. These forces often motivate people to give their lives to ideas and causes that deny the very existence of God and the infinite worth of human personality.

Christ came into a world much the same as ours. He taught truth about God, man, righteousness, and evil. Having revealed truth, he reconciled evil man to God. He dispelled fear and gave hope to the hopeless. He placed infinite value on human life. Jesus commissioned those to whom he gave life to share this source of life and truth with others.

One reason Christ established his church was to counter evil forces in the world. In fact, first-century Christians were often called revolutionists because of their evident intention to overthrow satanic powers. When Paul and Silas visited other Christians in Thessalonica, the Jews complained to the rulers: "These that have turned the world upside down are come hither also" (Acts 17:6). But as one has said, when Christians turn the world upside down, it is then right side up. Christ is continuing to establish and commission churches to enter into conflict with the evil forces that bring fear, hate, confusion, and rebellion to human life. Sharing his gospel is still man's hope for personal survival.

The challenge and opportunity of today demands that Southern Baptist churches be at their best. Questions are being raised on every hand as to the adequacy and relevance of churches in our present society. Some are calling for a renewal

3

in the churches. Such indictments are sure to continue through the next decade.

Should churches and their leaders give attention to these evaluations? Can churches which are brought into being by the act of God experience a renewal? Providing acceptable answers to these questions is the responsibility of churches and their leaders. In answering, a church must express itself in actions as well as words. An unbelieving world is best convinced by what it sees happening.

A church can best express itself to others when the members have a clear concept of whose they are and what they are to do. In other words, the meaning of a church's existence is wrapped up in its nature. How rich is the concept of a church held by members of Southern Baptist churches? Do they really understand what it is? What its purpose is? What it can become?

I. A Church—a Spiritual Organism

A church is primarily an organism by nature. This means it has life. A church is an organism because its life does not come from outside itself. Rather it has life because its source of life is within. The source of a church's life is the Spirit of Jesus Christ. Therefore, we can say that a church is a spiritual organism.

It is important for a church to understand that it is an organism with its source of life within. It is even more important for a church to be consciously aware of the life that is within. The presence of this life is recognized by members who are conscious of the true nature of a church.

1. *A Supernatural Creation*

Many organisms may be found in our world. Evidence is conclusive that physical organisms are a result of the natural creative processes of God. Not so with a church. It owes its existence to the supernatural activity of God. Every church member should continually remember that God through Jesus Christ left his heavenly place and came into the midst of mankind to redeem man and establish his church (Phil. 2:5–11).

As both God and man, Christ performed his mighty act of redemption through which man would never die or be in bondage (Romans 8). Through Jesus Christ, God made it possible for all men to become new creatures (2 Cor. 5 : 17). When they accept him, they become new creatures because Jesus Christ comes to live his life within them.

The supernatural work of God was accomplished once for all at Calvary. But in a real sense, the response of each new person to Jesus Christ is because of the supernatural work of God. After Peter's historic confession of belief that Jesus was the Messiah, Jesus reminded Peter (and disciples of all ages): "Blessed art thou, Simon Bar-jona: for flesh and blood hath not revealed it unto thee, but my Father which is in heaven. And I say also unto thee, That thou art Peter, and upon this rock I will build my church; and the gates of hell shall not prevail against it" (Matt. 16:17–18).

It was God who singled out Peter for this supernatural revelation. It was God who through the Holy Spirit revealed Jesus Christ as the source of this life to the three thousand at Pentecost. God's activity accounts for the existence of your church and mine.

2. A Community of Faith and Hope

A church is a community of persons who are spiritually alive and held together because of their faith. These persons have life because of their belief in a person. One at a time God adds to a church "such as should be saved" (Acts 2 : 47).

The center of the faith of all Christians is Jesus Christ. Around him gather the believers in a common faith. They believe the death and resurrection of Jesus Christ was an absolute necessity if persons were and are to have a new life. They believe that Christ now reigns as Lord of all life with all power in heaven and in earth given to him by God (Matt. 28 : 18). They believe that victory over all satanic forces has already been accomplished; the church has only to press the battle to overcome death and hell. They believe that the Christ who reigns at the right hand of God is also living his life today through the community of faith.

The vitality of a church as a spiritual organism is evidenced also by the hope that springs from within. Hope is evidence of life. The hope of a church surpasses the understanding of unbelievers. There is no trouble which can beset the Christian community which cannot be borne with Jesus Christ. There is no loneliness too great to bear, because every church has this friend within.

The persecution and curses of the world are but means by which believers test the hope of their salvation. Through hope, the daily struggles of human life are made holy experiences as a church lives out its life in service. The hope of the resurrection gives redeemed men courage to lay down their lives for their friends—and their enemies. Such hope is always a miracle to behold. Hope is characteristic of any church which is consciously aware of its nature as a spiritual organism. It is characteristic of a church which believes in the here and now fulfilment of the Lord's promise: "Lo, I am with you alway, even unto the end of the world" (Matt. 28:20).

Perhaps the greatest hope of a church is that with Christ it is facing a defeated enemy. Through the work of Jesus Christ, Satan has been overcome. So believers today can take hope that the same divine power that raised Christ from the dead is available for facing all of Satan's trials and tribulations.

3. *A Fellowship of Love*

The nature of an organism gives it a consciousness of being a unity. This conscious sense of oneness is commonly referred to as the fellowship of a church. The quality of this fellowship is characterized by the word "love." Not a human love which seeks at best to do unto others as you would have them do unto you. Rather it is a love shared with friend and foe alike as a means by which God can perform his redemptive work with others. The Greek word to describe this fellowship of love is *koinonia*.

The basis for *koinonia* in a church stems from the experience each member has had with God. Church members know that in their great moment of truth before God they stood as ragged beggars in need of the Bread of life. The redeemed of God, his church, can proclaim that no life is too sinful or too selfish to be excluded from the love of God. They, better than the world, know the meaning of Paul's words: "But God commendeth his love toward us, in that, while we were yet sinners, Christ died for us" (Rom. 5:8).

God loved us in spite of what we were; he loves us in spite of what we are. So in a church, the fellowship of love is not earned by righteousness or works or faith. It is the gift of God, along with salvation. He has given a church to believers as a haven from hate, envy, jealousy, and fear. So church members who accept one another for what they are need not erect barriers of prejudice, envy, pride, or hate. Through the power of the love of God, members of this organism can tear down those walls of dishonesty which keep men from sharing the fellowship of God. This kind of love redeems that which was lost.

The fellowship of a church is not the fruit of its purity or its faithfulness. It is the fruit of having Jesus Christ alive and active in the church.

II. A Church—an Organized Organism

Thus far the description of a church's nature has carefully avoided picturing the church as an organization. This has been purposefully done in order that a church may be seen for what it truly is—a living organism. But as an organism, a church exists in a form which has not changed and will not change until the end of the ages. This unchanging form is not to be thought of as the *organizations* of a church. It should be clearly seen as the unchangeable organization of the organism.

In describing the form of the organism, the most significant term used in the New Testament is "the body of Christ." Is this not logical since we have previously established the fact that Christ is the life of the church? There are other reasons which justify the use of the term "body of Christ" to describe the organized nature of the church.

Organized describes the whole form which results from the

arrangement of related parts. Notice in the illustration below how the pie-shaped parts are organized into a whole form.

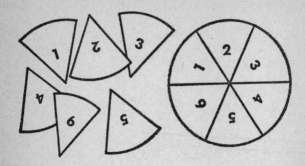

How does this apply to the nature of a church as an organized organism? The idea words "arrangement," "related parts," "entity," and "specific purpose" give us the clue.

1. Fashioned by God

Christ gave his life for the church. Paul says he took upon himself the form of a servant, humbled himself, and became obedient unto death. He performed his redemptive work in order that he might redeem unto himself a "chosen generation; a royal priesthood, an holy nation, a peculiar people . . . which in time past were not a people, but are now the people of God" (1 Peter 2:9–10).

From the redeemed, Christ declared he would build (in such a manner) his church so that even the gates of hell should not deter it from its purpose.

If we confidently believe the New Testament, then we accept as fact not only that God through Jesus Christ adds to his church but also that he adds to specific churches such as should be saved.

So God fashioned the church as an organism according to his pattern for it. "But now hath God set the members every one of them in the body, as it hath pleased him" (1 Cor. 12: 18). Through faith we can see that God in the fulness of time brings into churches those persons who can as members of his body achieve more perfectly the will of God for their individual lives as well as for the life of the fellowship. Church members should consciously observe that God is fashioning their church to make its unique contribution to the expansion and growth of the kingdom of God. Perception of how God is building a church can lead it to grasp significant and unique opportunities for advancing the kingdom of Christ.

2. *Consists of Related Parts*

A church consists of Christ, who is the head of the body, and believers, who are the members of the body.

The Christ who is the head of the body is not now on a cross. He is not now in a tomb. The head of the body is the living Lord. He is the head now. He functions to give the body direction, to think its thoughts, and to control its actions. How else could Paul have written, "For to me to live is Christ" (Phil. 1:21)? Or again in his letter to the Philippian church, "Let this mind be in you, which was also in Christ Jesus" (Phil. 2:5).

Believers constitute the members of the body. Each has his own particular responsibility to contribute to "effectual working in the measure of every part" (Eph. 4:16). According to God's plan, even though all are to be members, they are not to be identical. The body of Christ has need of new creatures who together possess a variety of gifts. Thus, they can perform the diversities of operations which are the responsibilities of the members of the body. "For the body is not one member, but many. If the foot shall say, Because I am not the hand, I am not of the body; is it therefore not of the body? And if the ear shall say, Because I am not the eye, I am not of the body; is it therefore not of the body? If the whole body were an eye, where were the hearing? If the whole were hearing, where were the smelling? But now hath God set the members every one of them in the body, as it hath pleased him. And if they were all one member, where were the body?" (1 Cor. 12:14–19). Even as the human body must add new cells to maintain growth and life, the church must continue to add members to its body for functioning growth.

The primary characteristic of the organized organism is its relatedness. The body of Christ consists of parts which because of their relationship give the body its unity. Actually, this unity of the body is the best evidence of the quality of life a church has. In other words, it reflects the degree to which the members are possessed by Christ. The visual evidence of this unity is in the love which the members have for one another (1 John 4:11–21). These relationships are the means by which the organism retains its wholeness. Without these supernatural relationships the body would fragment and disintegrate. W. O. Carver in commenting on this idea in the Scriptures wrote, "In the book of Ephesians Christ and the church are so intimately related as to constitute one entity, neither being complete except in relation to the other."

This leads to the conclusion that the body of Christ is one. Paul's description of this oneness is difficult to improve upon. "There is one body, and one Spirit, even as ye are called in one hope of your calling; one Lord, one faith, one baptism, one God and Father of all" (Eph. 4:4–6).

Thus we see that the very oneness of the body is the result of every part being and doing its part, every member fulfilling his responsibility; every part maintaining an intimate relationship to the head and to the other parts. "From whom the whole body fitly joined together and compacted by that which every joint supplieth, according to the effectual working in the measure of every part, maketh increase of the body unto the edifying of itself in love" (Eph. 4:16).

The relationship of the members to Jesus Christ determines its unity. This cohesive relationship is reflected in the singleness of purpose which the body receives from its head. If church members are to be true to the head, they must *live* the life of Christ in the world. Here then is the unifying factor which keeps the church in one accord. The members' being in accord with the head is the basis for receiving supernatural power to perform a church's work.

A church expresses its nature best when in oneness of purpose the members live in intimate relationship to the head and to one another.

CHAPTER 2

I. GOD'S UNCHANGING PURPOSE FOR A CHURCH
   1. To Be in Fellowship with Christ and to Minister in His Name
   2. To Love One Another
   3. To Bring All Men to Christ
   4. To Make Disciples of All Nations
   5. To Guide Christians in Growing Toward Christlikeness

II. THE FUNCTIONS OF A CHURCH
   1. To Worship
   2. To Proclaim
   3. To Educate
   4. To Minister

2

The Purpose and Functions
of a Church

W. O. CARVER has referred to churches as " 'colonies' of the kingdom of heaven on earth, located in the midst of the world which is to be won through the gospel. They are not only emigration centers for heaven but are also recruiting agencies and training instruments and supervising bodies for the recruits as they become active workers in the gospel." [1]

A church then does not have a purpose of its own—only God's purpose for it. Since Christ is the head of a church, the church's purpose is found in what Christ established his churches to do. A church's purpose is God's timeless unchanging intention for it. It is the reason Christ called it into being. As the term is used here, a church's purpose is synonymous with its mission.

It is important for every church member to understand as fully as possible God's purpose for his church. Man is finite, so it is difficult to understand fully what this purpose is. The Bible does not give an exact definition, but key passages provide clues which lead to new understandings of the purpose of a church.

I. GOD'S UNCHANGING PURPOSE FOR A CHURCH

Among numerous passages of Scripture which throw light on God's unchanging purpose for his church are Mark 4:14-15; John 13:34-35; Acts 1:8; Matthew 28:18-20; and

---

[1] W. O. Carver, "Introduction," *What Is the Church?*, ed. Duke K. McCall (Nashville: Broadman Press, 1958), p. 13.

Ephesians 4 : 11–13. Consider what these Scriptures reveal regarding the purpose of a church.

1. *To Be in Fellowship with Christ and to Minister in His Name*

It is interesting to note Jesus' purpose in calling the twelve disciples: "And he ordained twelve, that they should be with him, and that he might send them forth to preach, and to have power to heal sicknesses, and to cast out devils" (Mark 3 : 14–15).

According to this account by Mark, Jesus had a twofold purpose in appointing the twelve: that they might have fellowship with him and that he might send them out to represent him. Matthew elaborates on the type of ministry they were to perform. They were to heal the sick, raise the dead, and cleanse the lepers.

R. W. Kicklighter comments on Mark 3 : 14–15:

The Greek conjunction separating the two purposes makes the calling and fellowship point to the sending forth or mission of making other disciples, that is, the formation of a society. Jesus also established a covenant with the twelve at the Last Supper. This covenant, reminiscent of the Old Testament covenant at Mount Sinai, is clarified by the covenants of Isaiah 43 : 6–7 and 49 : 8–9 where the Servant is given for "a covenant with the people." This brief survey is sufficient to show that Jesus intended the formation of an exclusive, missionary community, and its formation has been shown to be the direct result of his Person and Ministry." [2]

2. *To Love One Another*

Christ gave his disciples a new commandment. They were to love one another. "A new commandment I give unto you, That ye love one another; as I have loved you, that ye also love one another. By this shall all men know that ye are my disciples, if ye have love one to another" (John 13 : 34–35). In this new commandment, Christ emphasized that the love of

[2] R. W. Kicklighter, "The Origin of the Church," *What Is the Church?* Duke K. McCall (Nashville: Broadman Press, 1958), p. 44.

the disciples for one another was not to be a token love. It was to have depth and quality. They were to love one another as Christ loved them. Actually, this was not possible. Christ stated his commandment in this way to stress the importance of Christians loving one another.

The disciples were to experience untold hardship, persecution, and even violent death. When Christ sent his disciples out, he warned, "Behold, I send you forth as sheep in the midst of wolves" (Matt. 10:16). Later when Christ's prophetic words came to pass, the disciples were sustained by the love of God, and by their love for one another. Since then, followers of Christ who have suffered persecution and who have been renounced by their families have found that their brothers and sisters in Christ love them even more than their own flesh and blood.

In giving the new commandment, Christ also told his disciples that their discipleship could be measured by their love for one another. They could not be his true followers if they did not love one another.

This commandment speaks as truly to the children of God today as in the day Christ gave it. Church members are to love one another even as New Testament disciples loved one another. Love for Christ and love for fellow church members should characterize Baptist church life today.

3. *To Bring All Men to Christ*

After his resurrection Jesus told his apostles, "But ye shall receive power, after that the Holy Ghost is come upon you: and ye shall be witnesses unto me both in Jerusalem, and in all Judaea, and in Samaria, and unto the uttermost part of the earth" (Acts 1:8).

Doubtless the apostles were concerned with receiving the kind of power for which the Roman government was famous. Their question (Acts 1:6) indicated their need of a new power to help them take the gospel to the world.

Jesus' reply was that the Holy Spirit would give them power as he came upon them. They would then become Christ's witnesses. The word for *witness* is the one from which comes our word "martyr." They were to witness to Christ even at the cost of their lives.

After the Holy Spirit came upon them, they were to be Christ's witnesses to the remotest part of the earth. Christ at one time commanded them to avoid Samaria (Matthew 10:5), but now they were to include it in their witness. Jesus on Olivet could point to Jerusalem, Judea, Samaria, and to the uttermost part of the earth. It was his desire that all men should hear the gospel.

In this discussion with his apostles, Jesus was making it clear that they were to proclaim the gospel to the remotest places of earth in order to bring all men into redemptive relationship with him. He summarized his purpose for his followers by declaring that they were to be his witnesses throughout the world.

4. *To Make Disciples of All Nations*

Further insight into the purpose of a church is found in the Great Commission: "Jesus came up and spoke to them, saying, 'All authority has been given to Me in heaven and on earth. Go therefore and make disciples of all the nations, baptizing them in the name of the Father and the Son and the Holy Spirit, teaching them to observe all that I commanded you; and lo, I am with you always, even to the end of the age'" (Matt. 28:18–20, NASB). In these words, the risen Christ proclaimed the worldwide mission of his church. His disciples were commissioned to make disciples (learners) of all nations. Not a person anywhere was to be excluded. Men of all nations were not only to be won to Christ but also to become learners even as Christ's followers were. They were to be taught by their churches, and this teaching was to be a continuing experience. They were to be taught until they observed what Christ had commanded his disciples to do.

The purpose of Christ's work on earth was not only to save men from sin but also to prepare them for intelligent, faithful service. Spiritual birth calls for spiritual growth under the skilled guidance of those who have been taught by the Master Teacher.

The Great Commission often is considered only in terms of missions overseas, but it speaks to every church, everywhere, in every generation. Its stress is on making disciples of all men.

5. *To Guide Christians in Growing Toward Christlikeness*

Paul in writing to the church at Ephesus (Eph. 4: 11–13) contributes further insights into the purpose of a church: "And he gave some, apostles; and some, prophets; and some, evangelists; and some, pastors and teachers; for the perfecting of the saints, for the work of the ministry, for the edifying of the body of Christ: till we all come in the unity of the faith, and of the knowledge of the Son of God, unto a perfect man, unto the measure of the stature of the fulness of Christ."

The work of these early churches called for leaders with various gifts of leadership. Apostles, prophets, evangelists, pastors, and teachers were needed. This work was to equip the saints for their work of service and to build up the body of Christ.

Christians have tasks to perform for which they need special preparation. When Christians perform their tasks under the lordship of Christ, they have a part in strengthening the church as a living fellowship. The ultimate end of this service is that "we all attain . . . to a mature man, to the measure of the stature which belongs to the fulness of Christ" (Eph. 4: 13, NASB). Winning lost men to Christ and guiding their spiritual growth after conversion is for the purpose of helping them to become like Christ.

All four classes of leadership mentioned in Ephesians are "gifts" of the risen, ascended, and administering Christ in order to develop a devoted, redeemed humanity. The functions of these four groups all tend primarily to the extension and the establishment of Christian centers in various geographical divisions. The first three have to do with bringing the gospel to new regions and helping those who receive it to begin Christian living. The work of "apostles, prophets, evangelists" prepares for, and culminates in, the work of "pastors and teachers" (two functions of the same group). These latter lead in the developing of the converts in their duties, their function, their organization, their Christian living "worthy of the gospel." Paul said that the function of each group looks to the equipment of all the saints for the work of ministering. The ultimate end is a continuous, harmonious, effective progress of the entire body, ever increasing in love as it becomes the "body of Christ." [3]

With these twelve apostles Jesus began the formal organization of his kingdom in the world. For this purpose the apostles were given a long period of close fellowship with Jesus. He also gave them instruction both public and private concerning himself, his kingdom, and his will for mankind. He gave them power and sent them forth to minister to persons in need.

The passages of Scripture referred to above show many similarities. Central in each is Christ's calling men to lives of full commitment and ministry. As men respond, they are given a new nature. They become Christ's disciples and serve him in relation to other disciples.

A church's principal concern should be finding and doing the will of Jesus Christ, who is the head of each church. "Each group of believers becomes in its own location the body of Christ. Each is 'distinctly a temple of God in the Holy Spirit' and is so sacred that whoever destroys it will himself be destroyed (1 Cor. 3:17). Its unity, its fellowship, its representative character is such that factions and divisions in that body divide Christ and bring his condemnation." [4]

Doing the will of Christ causes a church to be concerned to reach unreached persons for Christ. Not a concern simply that a church may count persons but that persons may count for Christ. Not just that men may experience spiritual birth but that they may also experience spiritual growth. "Evangelism . . . is one beggar telling another beggar where to get food." [5]

Christ loved persons enough to take the form of a person

[3] Carver, *op. cit.,* p. 3.

[4] *Ibid.,* p. 7.

[5] D. T. Niles, *That They May Have Life* (New York: Harper & Bros., 1951), p. 96.

and to live and die for all persons. Christ's followers should love Christ and persons enough to take the gospel of Christ to persons everywhere.

A church's primary concern then should be for persons—the person Jesus Christ and the relationship of all persons to him through saving faith.

Christ magnified these two relationships above all others in the Great Commandment: "Hear, O Israel; the Lord our God is one Lord: and thou shalt love the Lord thy God with all thy heart, and with all thy soul, and with all thy mind, and with all thy strength: this is the first commandment. And the second is like, namely this, Thou shalt love thy neighbour as thyself. There is none other commandment greater than these" (Mark 12:29–31).

What then is the purpose of a church? The purpose of a church is to be a fellowship of baptized believers in Jesus Christ, experiencing the love and discipleship of God, loving and sharing a common life with one another, and seeking to bring all men into these same relationships.

II. The Functions of a Church

The purpose of a church is understood further by studying the functions of a church. A function of a church is a basic kind of action which is consistent with the nature of the church. Note carefully what these functions are and how they relate to the nature and purpose of a church.

Confusion exists in many churches as to what the work of Christ is. The Master was not confused; the New Testament indicates clearly basic functions of a church. The will of God for a particular congregation at a particular time can, of course, be known only as that congregation seeks God's will through prayer. But the responsibility of a church which seeks to pattern itself after the New Testament can be found in the functions to worship, to proclaim, to educate, and to minister. These functions are not independent of one another. Rather, they are interrelated and interdependent. As the lungs, heart, brain, and digestive system are vital to human life, worship, proclamation, education, and ministry are essential to the life of a church. Poor functioning in any one of these areas means a weak and limited body. Healthy functioning results in the growth and the effective working of the body.

1. *To Worship*

To worship is to experience an awareness of God, to adore him in recognition of his holiness and majesty, and to respond in loving obedience to his leadership.

Essentially, a worship experience is concerned with the creation and sustenance of life. All men stand in awe of life and the creator of life. From the beginning of time, man has worshiped the sun, the moon, the rain, and all other elements to which he has attributed life-giving powers. Christian worship is directed to Jehovah God, the source of eternal life. "But God, who is rich in mercy, for his great love wherewith he loved us, even when we were dead in sins, hath quickened us together with Christ, (by grace ye are saved)" (Eph. 2:4–5).

Worship is truly the heart of a church. Through it a congregation keeps in touch with God, the giver of life. Love, praise, repentance, and commitment are all genuinely and vitally expressed. Worship becomes more than human fellowship. It is conscious personal fellowship with the personal God as revealed in Jesus Christ.

The church worships God through praise, thanksgiving, and adoration. Remembering the mighty acts of God in Christ Jesus and his continuing work through the centuries, the church sings joyfully to God. The congregation bows in grateful thanksgiving for the grace of God that has made this possible. It reviews the work that God has done in its own life through the years, during the past week, and during each day.

Through preaching and reading the Scriptures, a church evaluates its life. It ceases to be selfish; it is called to its true nature. A worshiping church is a giving church, for it is impossible to worship without committing oneself to God. In worship, the congregation offers its love, its praise, its life, and its work to God.

Because God is present, worship is more than giving by the congregation. God also gives through worship. He gives the church the necessary strength for its life. Through the obedient congregation, God shares his power for living and growing, for loving and going.

The particular form of congregational worship depends on each individual church. The essence of worship, however, is always characterized by several things: God is present and actively seeking a relationship with the congregation. The congregation is seeking to glorify God with one mind and one mouth (see Rom. 15:6). A worshiping congregation desires to know the truth in its deepest spiritual meaning. The Lord spoke of such worship when he said: "But the hour cometh, and now is, when the true worshippers shall worship the Father in spirit and in truth: for the Father seeketh such to worship him. God is a Spirit: and they that worship him must worship him in spirit and in truth" (John 4:23-24).

Worship calls for response on the part of the congregation. Many congregations are willing to watch the pastor and musicians perform. Often they sit waiting to see what will happen. But when the body of Christ is worshiping, every member makes a response to God. Singing is more than singing with the director or minister of music and the choir; it is singing to God. Praying is more than listening to the prayer leader; it is the entire congregation putting concern into the meaning of every word spoken. Listening to the sermon is more than listening to a preacher; it is seeking the truth of God through his revealed Word. Many church members leave worship services tired from sitting rather than refreshed from worshiping.

Worship is never consummated until the worshiper serves. Obedient response is the essential factor for judging the quality of a worship experience. "Thy will be done in earth, as it is in heaven" (Matt. 6:10) is the response of every person who has truly worshiped. Thus worship is foundational to the church's effective witness in its immediate community and throughout the world.

2. *To Proclaim*

To proclaim the gospel is to declare what God has done in and through Jesus Christ for the salvation of men.

Evangelism is confronting unbelievers with the news that God has provided redemption from sin through Jesus Christ. Churches which fail to declare this news are as branches that bear no fruit. In addition to witnessing to the unsaved, a church must deal with the doubts of church members until they "grow up in all aspects into Him, who is the head, even Christ" (Eph. 4:15, NASB).

Preaching is a primary means for proclaiming the gospel of salvation to the lost. Preaching the gospel must take place where unbelievers are. Therefore, churches may need to reconsider their concept of preaching in order to reach those who do not come to the church building seeking God and salvation.

Proclaiming by a church is more than the preaching of the pastor. Every church member has a responsibility to fulfil this function. Personal witnessing about Jesus Christ is the day-to-day means by which a church proclaims. The content of the proclaimed message to our world is what God did in Jesus Christ, what Jesus Christ has done for men, and what God is doing today. Every person who has experienced salvation should be an evangel of God's grace.

The need of the world has not changed. Satan still dominates the hearts and lives of millions of persons. As evil abounds, there is a greater need for the proclamation of the good news. The preacher is the member with the major preaching responsibility, but the congregation cannot expect the preacher alone to proclaim the gospel to unbelievers. The preacher who must single-handedly evangelize his community faces an almost impossible task. In addition, the church must invest in the missionary enterprise in the association, state, nation, and world.

Many congregations have excused themselves from their responsibility in evangelism. The New Testament teaches that all the members are to function as personal witnesses. Christ has not yet withdrawn his command for believers to be his witnesses. Churches must look anew at this function. They must develop the New Testament habit of sharing Christ each day.

3. *To Educate*

To educate is to lead persons to the knowledge and acceptance of Jesus Christ as Saviour and Lord, to teach and train the church's constituency to perform the functions of their churches, and to help them develop toward full Christian maturity.

Persons may be taught concepts of the Christian life before they accept Christ. However, education in the Christian life begins with the conversion experience. Learning is essential to the growth of every redeemed person. Education is the process by which persons grow in understanding, form new attitudes, and develop actions consistent with the example of Christ. This learning is aided by the work of the Holy Spirit.

Christian growth is dependent on the processes of learning, just as physical growth is dependent upon the digestive processes. However, recognition must be given to God's supernatural action which often accomplishes results in a moment where education would require a lifetime. Christ set the example for a church in education. He spent much of his time teaching. His invitation to the multitudes was: "Take my yoke upon you, and learn of me; for I am meek and lowly in heart: and ye shall find rest unto your souls" (Matt. 11:29).

It was the pattern of the New Testament churches to educate. All those who were added to the church were expected to "continue steadfastly in the apostles' doctrine" until they had been stabilized in the Christian faith and life. Paul urged the Colossian Christians to walk "rooted and built up in him [Christ], and stabilized in the faith," as they had been taught (Col. 2:7). The clearest evidence that a person is growing toward Christian maturity is the searching mind, seeking for the truth of God. The words of Christ "Ye shall know the truth, and the truth shall make you free" should cause every church to undertake its educational function with renewed strength and purpose.

Through education, Baptist churches learn how to be better churches. Each church is a school. It educates in an informal and in a formal manner. This statement recognizes that much of the education of a church takes place in the life situations of the congregation, for every action of a congregation has in it educational consequences. It is the responsibility of the congregation to see that education, informal and formal, contributes to significant learning experiences on the part of its members.

Since much learning takes place outside the church and its classrooms, the congregation should look upon such experiences as birth, death, marriage, and sickness as particularly valuable opportunities for Christian education.

In order to be sure that learning is meaningful, Baptist churches need to identify the content areas which they must carry on. A content area is any basic area of content which requires continuing study on the part of the congregation in order for the church to achieve its objectives. The content areas of a church must provide opportunities for the congregation to learn about every aspect of the Christian faith and life. The studies must provide depth that will stabilize the believer thoroughly in the faith. They should also prepare him to live as a world citizen.

4. *To Minister*

To minister is to make a loving response to the needs of persons in Jesus' name.

Many times during his ministry Jesus' body was tired and exhausted. On more than one occasion it was necessary for him to withdraw from the multitudes to seek a place of solitude. No man has ever lived who had the compassion or who felt the suffering of mankind as did Jesus. Day after day of his short life was spent ministering to the sick, the lame, the sad, and the hungry.

Jesus set a clear standard by which a person may measure importance or status as a member of the body of Christ: "But whosoever will be great among you, let him be your minister; and whosoever will be chief among you, let him be your servant: even as the Son of man came not to be ministered unto, but to minister, and to give his life a ransom for many" (Matt. 20:26–28).

As congregations grow, it becomes easier for the members to be insensitive to the suffering, loneliness, and physical needs of fellow members. With community welfare agencies undertaking more and more social action, churches tend to surrender their function of ministry to them. Congregations must awaken to the consequence of ignoring Christ's warning about the final judgment. Read Matthew 25:42–46, and consider especially these words: "For I was an hungred, and ye gave me no meat: I was thirsty, and ye gave me no drink: I was a stranger, and ye took me not in: naked, and ye clothed me not: sick, and in prison, and ye visited me not. Then shall they also answer him, saying, Lord when saw we thee an hungred, or athirst, or a stranger, or naked, or sick, or in prison, and did not minister unto thee? Then shall he answer them, saying, Verily I say unto you, Inasmuch as ye did it not to one of the least of these, ye did it not to me."

A church as the body of Christ should follow his example. It must ask itself what it will do about the hunger and suffering of the world. Congregations must learn to suffer with mankind wherever suffering takes place. This means that churches should cooperate in sharing the burdens of men of every race in every nation of our world. Giving gifts to be used by others in missionary enterprises is not enough. Churches must share personally the common life struggle of all men.

Ministry may be expressed individually or collectively. In ministering individually, a person may seek to meet the physical need of someone, as did the good Samaritan. Or he may seek to meet a spiritual need, as Jesus did in personal witness to the woman at the well. Individual ministry may be expressed as members engage in personal or group counseling or as they visit in homes.

Collective ministering may be expressed in such actions as sharing clothes with the needy or food with the hungry. A church may make benevolent responses to those who are homeless, financially distressed, or transient. Collective ministry may be expressed in attention to special groups with particular needs, such as language groups, racial groups, military personnel, or students.

Chapter 1 and this chapter present the church as an organism—its nature, purpose, and functions. Understanding the biblical concepts of these two chapters is the key to understanding the other chapters of the book. Before proceeding to chapter 3, scan quickly the first two chapters. Link them together to understand more clearly your church as the body of Christ with Christ as its head. Ask yourself: What is God's purpose for my church? What are my church's basic kinds of actions? What do these answers mean to me as a church member?

CHAPTER 3

3

Organizing the Work of a Church

"I MUST WORK the works of him that sent me, while it is day: the night cometh, when no man can work" (John 9:4). When Jesus said that he must "work the works" of the one who had sent him, he meant just that. He committed this work to his disciples, and he established the church to continue this work until he returned to earth. (Read John 14:10–13.)

I. ORGANIZING THE WORK OF A CHURCH

The purpose and functions of a church require it to act. The purpose sets forth the ultimate end of all actions. The functions describe the kinds of actions which are consistent with the church's nature. But to have a purpose and to have functions is not the same as taking action. Action is the means by which work is done—the means for achieving a church's purpose.

Most church members are ready for their church to accept its full responsibility for carrying on the work of Christ in the world. The difficulty lies in identifying that work which a church should do. There is more church work to be done than can ever be done. There is also great diversity in the work to be done within the limits of a church's functions. A church needs to organize its work in order to carry it out effectively. Perhaps a review of the statement on "organizing" on page 7 will be helpful at this point.

Because the organizational work of a church is so often misunderstood, the following discussion shows how this work actually emerges from the nature, purposes, and functions of a church. To illustrate the principle, the presentation begins

27

as if a church had no established organization. However, as the ideas unfold, familiar expressions begin to appear.

1. *Identifying the Tasks*

Work consists primarily of carrying on activities. Identifying activities is, therefore, the beginning point in organizing. How can a church identify its actions in order to determine the working relationships for its members? The job seems impossible when one considers the numerous activities a church performs. However, it becomes a possibility if approached a step at a time.

The first step is to identify those activities which are basic and continuing. By limiting the organizing job in the beginning to identifying these activities, one can form a clearer picture. When looked at in its simplest form, work can more easily be related properly to all the activities which eventually emerge. The words "basic" and "continuing" offer a clue to identifying the simplest expression of activities. Webster defines the words as follows:

Basic—relating to or forming the base.
Continuing—marked by uninterrupted extension in space or time; needing no renewal.

Thus, a church should identify an activity as basic and continuing when it is performed on an uninterrupted or ongoing basis and when it forms a broad base for many other detailed activities of the church. For easy communication, such basic, continuing activities are referred to as tasks. A task is thus understood to be a basic continuing activity, the performance of which is necessary to assist a church in achieving its purpose. A simple but comprehensive statement of tasks is illustrated by the list below.

CHURCH TASKS

a. Preach to believers and unbelievers
b. Reach the church's prospects
c. Teach and train the church's constituency to be a better church and to perform the church's functions

d. Lead church members to perform the church's functions at home and abroad
e. Provide information and resources needed in performing a church's functions
f. Provide the administrative means by which a church can perform its functions

2. *Organizing the Types of Tasks*

From the broad list of church tasks a more detailed list emerges. As each of these is classified according to its importance in moving a church toward its objectives, a more meaningful organization unfolds.

The word "importance" takes on a special meaning as used here. It does not mean that there are tasks "of no value or weight." Instead, the term is used to indicate that tasks of more than one order of importance exist. This evaluation is necessary if a church is to judge some tasks as having greater value than others in its life and work.

One way of organizing tasks for assignment is classifying them as church program tasks, church program service tasks, and administrative service tasks.

(1) *Church program tasks.*—These are the basic, continuing activities which are of primary importance in moving a church toward its objectives. They are characterized by their functional nature. In other words, program tasks are the kinds which grow directly out of the Great Commission. They are the direct actions of worship, proclamation, education, and ministry. Below is an illustration of program tasks emerging from church tasks a, b, c, d on page 28–29.

CHURCH PROGRAM TASKS

Preach to believers and unbelievers
Reach the church's prospects
Teach the constituency
  The biblical revelation
  Systematic theology
  Christian ethics
  Christian history
  Baptist polity and organization

Missions
Christian hymnody and music
Train the constituency in performing the church functions as
    members and leaders
Lead church members in performing the church's functions
    to the church as the body of Christ
    for the immediate community of the church
    for men of all nations

(2) *Church program service tasks.*—These are the basic,
continuing activities which churches perform to support the
carrying out of the program tasks. In other words, they serve
church leaders and members performing program tasks. Program service tasks are basic, continuing activities of secondary
importance in achieving a church's objectives. Below is an
illustration of church program service tasks.

CHURCH PROGRAM SERVICE TASKS

Provide and interpret information regarding the life and work
    of the church and the denomination
Procure, care for, and circulate resource materials
Program the use of audio-visuals and train leaders to use audio-
    visual materials and equipment
Determine recreation capacities of church members, plan a pro-
    gram of recreation activities, and assist church organizations
    in recreation activities

(3) *Administrative service task.*—Another type of task
consists of the basic, continuing actions of administration
which serve the congregation and its leaders. Administrative
actions provide the means needed by leaders to conduct their
work. These, too, are of secondary importance in achieving
a church's objectives. The difference between program service
and administrative service tasks will be illustrated in chapter
10.

A time may come when some great task in a program cannot be done because a program service or administrative
service task has not been performed. At that time, the performance of this program service or administrative service
task becomes of paramount importance. This does not, how-

ever, change the nature of the task into a church program task. A church should note the essential nature of every task, regardless of its natural importance in achieving the objectives of a church. The nature and the relationships of tasks require planning so that the performance of all necessary tasks will be done in proper sequence. Below is an illustration of task f.

ADMINISTRATIVE SERVICE TASK

Provide church organization, leadership, facilities, finances, and administrative controls

II. GROUPING THE TASKS FOR ASSIGNMENT TO PROGRAMS AND SERVICES

Organizing is never complete until permanent assignment of work has been made. Therefore, tasks should be organized for assignment to organization units of a church. In this step, programs and services are created. A program or service is formed by grouping one or more tasks. A program or service may be constituted of tasks from more than one classification.

There is no absolute right way to group and assign tasks to programs and services. Perhaps the principle of grouping similar tasks provides the best basis for making judgments. Tasks are judged to be similar when they have a common purpose in such things as type of work to be done, location of work, people to be served, work processes required, equipment or materials used, or sequence of actions to be taken.

The experience of Baptist churches in organizing has led to the natural application of the above principle. As a result, many programs and services are established already in the churches. Church members have not always realized that this work is church work; nevertheless, it is. Using the above listings of program and service tasks and the principle of grouping similar tasks, a church may state, group, and assign tasks in the following manner:

THE CONGREGATIONAL PROGRAM

1. Participate in the church's functions
2. State objectives and needs

3. Establish programs, program services, and administrative services
4. Provide for coordination of programs and services
5. Select and state responsibilities of the pastor and other leaders
6. Provide resources and means for achieving the church's objectives
7. Review regularly the life and work of the church in terms of its objectives

THE PASTORAL PROGRAM

1. Preach to believers and unbelievers
2. Lead the church to perform its functions
3. Give leadership to employed leaders
4. Perform pastoral responsibilities in the church's functions
5. Lead the deacons as they assist in performing pastoral responsibilities

THE SUNDAY SCHOOL PROGRAM

1. Teach the biblical revelation
2. Lead in reaching all prospects for the church
3. Lead all church members to worship, witness, learn, and minister daily
4. Provide organization and leadership for special projects of the church
5. Provide and interpret information regarding the work of the church and the denomination

THE BROTHERHOOD PROGRAM

1. Teach missions to all men, young men, and boys
2. Lead all men, young men, and boys to participate in missions activities
3. Provide organization and leadership for special missions projects of the church
4. Provide and interpret information regarding the work of the church and the denomination

THE WOMAN'S MISSIONARY UNION PROGRAM

1. Teach missions
2. Lead persons to participate in missions
3. Provide organization and leadership for special missions projects of the church

4. Provide and interpret information regarding the work of the church and the denomination

THE CHURCH MUSIC PROGRAM

1. Provide music and musicians for the congregational services and the organizations of the church
2. Lead persons to participate in hymn singing
3. Teach music and hymnody
4. Train persons to lead, sing, and play music
5. Provide organization and leadership for special projects of the church
6. Provide and interpret information regarding the work of the church and the denomination

THE TRAINING UNION PROGRAM

1. Teach systematic theology, Christian history, Christian ethics, and church polity and organization
2. Train church members to worship, witness, learn, and minister daily
3. Give orientation to new church members
4. Train leaders for the church and the denomination
   (1) Discover, recruit, and train potential leaders
   (2) Provide for specialized leader training
5. Provide organization and leadership for special projects of the church
6. Provide and interpret information regarding the work of the church and the denomination

THE CHURCH COUNCIL

1. Formulate and recommend to the congregation suggested church objectives and goals
2. Develop and recommend to the congregation strategies for reaching church goals
3. Review and coordinate suggested program plans and actions by church officers, organizations, and committees; and provide for adequate communication among church officers, organizations, and committees
4. Review and report as appropriate to the congregation the use of resources in terms of the needs of church programs as they work toward the achievement of the objectives and goals of a church

5. Evaluate program achievements in terms of church objectives and goals and report evaluations to the congregation

Because many churches have created so many organizations for carrying out program and administrative service tasks, it is not possible to list them here. Chapter 10 gives a detailed list of some of the tasks.

Thus far the discussion has shown how organizing proceeds from the simple to the complex in a logical, unfolding process. The example below uses the Sunday School and the Woman's Missionary Union programs and the library service to illustrate this process.

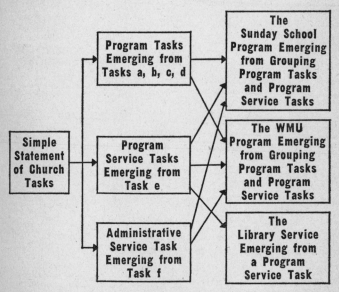

When the last stage of organizing the work has been reached, the church is then ready for its programs and services to begin programing and performing assigned work on a continuing basis.

III. PROGRAMING THE WORK OF A CHURCH

Since a church is God's creation, established to achieve his purpose, its work should be the most effective in the community. Effective spiritual work has its human, as well as its divine, side. Although led by the Spirit of God, a church has many adversaries. Therefore, it should plan and conduct its work well.

1. *A Plan for Programing*

A church can be helped by a reliable plan which provides stability, balance, and sequence for programing its work. Such a plan should include all essential aspects of programing in proper relation to one another. In other words, all that a church does in planning and working should be cared for in the plan.

The following eleven aspects form such a plan.

> Biblical foundations
> Philosophy (Policy)
> Objectives
> Church and community needs
> Program plan
> Relationships
> Organization
> Leaders-members
> Facilities
> Finances
> Administrative controls

The following is an interpretation of the above aspects.

(1) *Biblical foundations.*—By "biblical foundations" is meant a statement of biblical teachings which are believed to be foundational to a church's programing and planning.

The statement of biblical foundations is an expression of a church's beliefs. It is a church's conviction about the ultimate truth of life as revealed in the Bible. The statement provides a church at the first stage of the plan an opportunity to express its essential beliefs. The process of thinking through these beliefs should lead to improved understanding of, and appreciation for, what a church is and what it should become. It should provide basic direction for the thinking and decision-making of those who program and plan. Often conclusions from such statements are included in a church's constitution and covenant. Chapters 1 and 2 are an attempt to present a biblical basis for a church's programing and planning.

(2) *Philosophy.*—A church's philosophy is a statement of concepts which serves as a guide in conducting a church's programs.

A church's biblical foundations, significant historical events, and present situations determine why it organizes and operates as it does. The statement of philosophy reflects the concepts and principles, derived from the theology and the history of a church, which guide in organizing the operation of a church. This statement is an expression of the wisdom of a church. One person has defined the philosophy of a church as theology and experience put down into the here and now.

The process of thinking through a church's programing philosophy should establish firmly in the mind of the church leader those concepts and principles of a church which must not be violated.

Usually a church states its philosophy as policy. Policy is communicated in specific policies and procedures. Some of these may be included as a part of the constitution and covenant.

(3) *Objectives.*—Objectives are statements of a church's intention. They are statements of what a church intends to be and to accomplish on an ongoing basis. They seek to reflect God's eternal purpose in the church's contemporary situation.

As used in current programing, the overarching objective is a statement of intention to achieve something which can never be fully attained. It is a timeless intention. It serves as a North Star to those who are programing for churches.

The overarching objective is a statement of timeless intention to act in accordance with an unchanging purpose (established by congregation on recommendation from church council).

Areas of work are statements of intention to achieve balanced results from work within the range of functional activity (established by congregation on recommendation of church council).

Examples of how an overarching objective and area may be stated are given below:

The Overarching Objective

This is the way one church stated its great or overarching objective: To become increasingly aware of the church's relationship to God through Christ, to sustain a vital relation to him, and to be used of God to bring all men into this same relationship.

Areas of Work

Areas which might be chosen are:

Reaching new church members
Establishing new churches and missions
Ministering to persons of special needs
Increasing gifts to world missions advance
Increasing the individual usefulness of church members
Preparing for richer worship experiences

Objectives and areas serve as guides in preparing, analyzing, and selecting goals, strategies, and actions.

(4) *Church and community needs.*—Needs are common to all persons and groups of persons. The identified needs of people become the opportunities of service for a church. Seizing certain opportunities is inherent in God's instructions to his churches. These opportunities require that certain tasks be continually performed for a church's constituency and community. For example, teaching the biblical revelation must continue throughout the ages. Opportunities call for changes to be made in a church's present way of programing its tasks. New kinds of materials or teaching methods may become necessary.

A church does not have to identify all the church and community needs inherent in its particular situation. Neither does it have to identify new kinds of tasks nor materials to meet these needs. Southern Baptist churches and their denominational agencies have worked together over a period of years to develop new types and materials for meeting a large number of these opportunities.

A church may not be able to list all the opportunities its programs and services might discover from its community needs. The most important thing is for a church to identify regularly those which will most influence the future of its programs. In other words, it should identify those opportunities requiring new kinds of actions and materials which the church must have in order to meet significant needs not previously met.

(5) *Program (or service) plan.*—In the first part of this chapter are illustrations of how tasks can be organized into programs and services. The establishment of programs and services gives a church the *base* of the program plan. It provides a stable foundation from which specific actions that move toward achievement of objectives can be planned. Once this base has been approved by the church, it fades into the background. The planning of details becomes paramount.

The specific actions which will be carried out at specific times must be identified and brought together into a cohesive plan of action.

This part of the program plan consists of church goals, strategies, and detailed actions to be used in moving a church toward its objectives. In the plan, the program and service actions are listed in the order to be performed and assigned a specific date for performance.

Goals and strategies are defined as follows:

Goals are statements of intention to accomplish a measurable quantity and/or quality of results by a specified time (established by congregation upon recommendation of church council).

Strategy is a natural pattern of essential actions used in achieving a goal (established by church council on recommendation of individual program leaders).

An example of a goal and strategies growing out of the objective and areas on page 37 is as follows:

Goal

A goal under the area "Reaching New Church Members" may be stated this way: Our goal is to have increased our

church membership to _____ by _____.
     (number)   (exact date)

Strategy

Strategies for achieving the goal listed above may be:

A. Reaching new church members through Sunday School growth;

B. Reaching new church members through worship services and revivals; and

C. Reaching new church members through special mission action.

Any church can carry on activities in performing a task. However, not all activities make an essential and efficient contribution to achieving a church's objectives. In developing a dated plan of action, effort is made to select those activities which make an essential and efficient contribution to the successful performance of each task. This part of the program plan is the essence of effective programing. The evaluation of alternative plans of actions should result in eliminating the nonessential actions, balancing actions among key areas of work, adding actions where obvious gaps appear, and developing new kinds of activity to replace activity which has become ineffective.

Appropriate program and service action plans will be discussed in later chapters on programs and services.

(6) *Relationships.*—This aspect provides for the planning of all those relationships which are external to the church. They include relationships to the association, state convention, Southern Baptist Convention, other Baptist bodies, and community institutions and organizations. Inside the church it includes the agreed-upon relationships among program, program service, and administrative service organizations. The statements should include *what* relates the groups, *how* they relate, and *when* they relate.

(7) *Organization.*—Organization is the orderly arrangement of leaders and members to one another according to their assigned responsibilities in carrying out the program of a

church. It is the way a church groups its members to perform the assigned work.

A church must organize its work and its people if it is to conduct its work on an ongoing basis. Otherwise, it will fail to assign responsibility for conducting its program. In this plan for programing, the preceding aspects are concerned with *why* a church should organize itself and *what* it should organize to do. The steps in the plan for programing indicate that a church must first determine its essential work and then establish organizations to perform it. A church must express itself to itself and to the world. The means for expressing itself is organization.

Organization once established can be adjusted or adapted according to opportunities which a particular church program may have. Organization must never be so rigid that it cannot be changed to meet the changed needs of a church.

(8) *Leaders-members.*—This phase of planning is concerned with properly utilizing the human resources of a church. Manpower combines the ideas in this term, for it is the power available from, or supplied by, the physical and mental effort of man—in the case of a church, its leaders and members. Manpower programing consists of the following: discovering and recruiting persons for specific assignments in organizations, enlisting these workers in specific jobs, assisting them in getting adjusted in their work, giving them specialized training if needed, and guiding them as they serve.

Churches must ever be mindful of the truth of these words: "Not by might, nor by power, but by my spirit, saith the Lord of hosts" (Zech. 4 : 6). But under the leadership of the Spirit, human beings can do God's work. Churches must plan how their members can best be used in doing this.

(9) *Facilities.*—The dictionary defines a "facility" as a thing that promotes ease of action. Facilities, therefore, may be interpreted to mean the supplies, equipment, and buildings which promote ease of operation in the church's program. This gives a broad base to this aspect of the framework. Many things promote ease of action in a church's program. Buildings, teaching equipment, study materials, and record systems are

historic examples. Planning for the future in this field is limitless.

(10) *Finances*.—The financial phase provides for planning a church's financial resources. Finances are the monetary resources required to carry on the church's program. The process of this planning is generally concerned with budgeting.

A budget is the instrument by which the congregation controls its financial resources. This does not control in the sense of keeping costs within narrow limits. It means applying church income to the best advantage in accordance with need and in keeping with responsibility for current and future program development.

The budget is a reflection of the objectives and goals of a church. It is a description of how the goals are to be met. It is a congregation's commitment and authorization to carry out actions to attain established goals. The budget is a "costing out" of the program plans of a church. It is a tabulation of the dollar expenditures considered necessary to accomplish the work of a church and the anticipated income from which those expenditures will be met.

(11) *Administrative controls*.—Administrative controls are the means by which the church's program is controlled in accordance with church policy and procedures.

This aspect provides for planning and establishing the "controls" to be used. It is concerned with creating such things as policies and procedures, objectives, duties, program and budget reports. Controls imply the "right to exercise power." The communication and exercise of this authority is made more effective through good tools.

A church should program according to a sequence similar to that outlined above. Its work should be based on sound biblical foundations. Its objective should be clearly stated. It should identify and approve its programs and services. Its programs should have organization to conduct them. In this way, the ends toward which work is done come before the means by which work is done. Gradually the relationship of ends to means becomes clearer.

Church leaders should work step by step through the plan

for programing from biblical foundations to administrative controls. However, new insights gained in an aspect often call for restatements of aspects already complete. Work, then, is really "up and down" the plan, even though work logically flows downward from the first to the eleventh aspect of the plan.

2. *Principles of Church Programing*

As a church plans its tasks in detail, certain principles should be followed. There are at least five of these, all of which are important and interrelated.

PRINCIPLE 1—The church is the basic unit in all programing.

Christ intends for his churches to accomplish his work. He has given each church the same purpose. If this purpose is made clear to church members, they most likely will be filled with a sense of mission.

In programing its work, a church must begin with the church itself. It must be a whole church, not a fragmented one. It must be a church with a single purpose. The time has come to think of the church in these terms instead of only one or more of its organizations.

The Southern Baptist Convention's Committee on Correlation stated in 1937 that the "church is central and supreme." This is a valid statement, and it reinforces the principle of a church's being basic in all programing.

This first principle applies not only to programing the work of the church itself but also to the programing work of associations, state conventions, and the Southern Baptist Convention. Churches are and should be kept central in each of these programs. Those responsible for planning associational, state convention, and Southern Baptist Convention programs should keep in mind that their programs are but specialized extensions of the churches' programs. Denominational agencies carry forward the work of churches where churches as such cannot make their best contributions by acting individually.

PRINCIPLE 2—Church organization exists to carry out church tasks.

A church should first state its tasks, then group its tasks into programs, program services, and administrative services. Next it should organize its members to conduct these programs.

The program precedes and determines the organization. Organization is a means, not the end purpose. When a program is determined, an organization should be established to carry out the program. The logic and the sequence of these events mean that all organization within a church exists for doing *church* work.

Since the term "organization" in Baptist churches is applied to such types of organization as the Sunday School, Training Union, Woman's Missionary Union, Brotherhood, and Music Ministry, these are commonly thought of when the word "organization" is used. However, it is correct to refer to any grouping of persons to do church work as an organization. For example, the deacons are a church organization. Church committees also are organizations. In the term "church organization," every organized unit of the church's life is included. This means that any organization in a church should be for the purpose of carrying out church tasks.

PRINCIPLE 3—All tasks of the church program organizations should be programed and planned in relationship with other organizations.

It would be more nearly correct to say that all tasks of the church should be programed. This, of course, is necessary if a church is to do all of its essential work.

However, since church tasks of primary importance in moving a church toward its objectives are assigned to the church program organizations, this principle stresses the necessity of first relating these organizations. The assignments given to the church program organizations call for proper supporting actions on the part of program and administrative service organizations. For example, a church that is not reaching people can hold its Sunday School responsible, because its task is to lead in reaching all prospects for the church. If the Sunday School is fulfilling its responsibility in outreach, then the church can evaluate the mission actions being taken by Woman's Missionary Union, the Brotherhood, and the missions committee in keeping with their respective assignments.

If these organizations have programed their tasks of outreach properly, then the church can evaluate the training tasks of the Music Ministry and Training Union to determine whether these organizations are giving proper support to the task of outreach.

Church program organizations now are found in most churches. If not, such organizations can easily be established and utilized. Suggestions regarding assignments, constituency, organization, leadership, curriculum, and scheduled meetings for these organizations are readily available to churches. The educational tasks of the church program organizations are foundational to all that a church does. Their other tasks are related directly to these educational tasks. Church program organizations make learning more effective since they involve their members in applying what has been learned through study. Once a church has assigned all of its work for implementation, it is imperative that it devise some way to make certain that each of its basic actions is carried out continually and effectively. A church should see that each organization does its work. When an organization is assigned church work, the organization should program that work and conduct it. If this is not done, the church will fail to function as it should.

PRINCIPLE 4—A church program organization's relationship to a church's objectives determines the program organization's position in the church's plan of organization.

In the past, each church program organization took a unilateral approach to its work. Each programed its work and conducted it more or less independently of other organizations. Under such a pattern, the relationships of the various church organizations were never fully defined or understood. It was impossible to correlate and coordinate their work. Relationships are much clearer now, and the unilateral approach can be changed. When organizations are related properly, more thrust is provided for accomplishing all tasks.

The church program organizations should always act in keeping with their relationships to one another. These relationships vary according to the work to be done. In order for a church to function with maximum effectiveness in achieving a specific goal, it is necessary to establish a priority among tasks as the criteria for relating the organizations to one another.

For example, a priority area is to increase the usefulness of church members. A task of the church is to *lead church members to worship, witness, learn, and minister daily*. This is a priority task because it contributes to the spiritual growth of church members. Because of the program and organization of the Sunday School, this task is assigned to it. However, the Sunday School needs the support of other church organizations in carrying out the assignment. It can do its work far more effectively if the other organizations relate certain of their tasks to this Sunday School task. The Brotherhood and Woman's Missionary Union can give special attention to how these functions relate to mission study and mission actions. The Music Ministry can assist by training and leading members to participate with music.

The Training Union can train church members to worship, witness, learn, and minister daily. The Training Union can discover, recruit, and train potential leaders to guide in these functions in the future; and all organizations can provide specialized leadership training in order to improve the effectiveness of their present leaders.

In the tasks of outreach and leading in performing the church's functions, the Sunday School is given the lead position because its tasks make it primarily responsible to the church and because it can apply the church's maximum force through these tasks.

There are other church goals which cause the program organizations to relate differently. An illustration is the special mission offering goals which most churches set annually. These offerings, known as the Lottie Moon Christmas Offering and the Annie Armstrong Offering, were originally conducted by Woman's Missionary Union only. This fourth principle of programing, however, has proved that when the other four church program organizations support Woman's Missionary Union in informing church members about the offering, more persons are enlisted in giving, and mission gifts are increased. In this relationship, Woman's Missionary Union takes the lead, and it is supported by the Brotherhood, Sunday School, Training Union, and Music Ministry. Assembly programs on missions are recommended in both Sunday School and Training Union on the second Sunday of each of these weeks. These actions, in support of actions taken by Woman's Missionary Union and Brotherhood, serve to inform and motivate church members to participate worthily in the opportunities to learn, pray, and give.

This fourth principle of programing indicates how church organizations can be used to apply the proper force to the tasks of a church. The tendency has been to think of a church organization as always functioning in a fixed position. This concept makes the organization of the church too rigid to be of maximum effectiveness. A church needs to determine what its most important goals are. Then it should use its total organization to bring the greatest possible force into action to achieve these goals. Power is generated through properly relating organizations in order to get work done. Any church that will learn how to relate its organizations to do its work will accomplish far more than under any other system of operation.

PRINCIPLE 5—A church needs a strategy for properly relating assistance which it receives from the association, the state convention, and the Southern Baptist Convention. For this reason, these Baptist bodies should work together in developing this strategy.

There are associational programs, state convention programs, and Southern Baptist Convention programs, as well as church programs. These are created to assist churches in working together cooperatively. For example, there are four Sunday School programs: church, associational, state convention, and Southern Baptist Convention. Each of these programs is different, but the church program is at the heart of the other three. The programs of a church must be known before associational, state convention, and Southern Baptist Convention programs can be known and stated.

In historical actions, the churches established programs in

the associations, state conventions, and the Southern Baptist Convention to assist them to do their work. Activities multiply and organization pyramids when these programs are planned and conducted independently of one another and without first considering the content and needs of church programs.

In such a situation, a church may find itself having to maintain not only its own program but also program and organization for these additional programs without receiving adequate assistance from them.

These five principles of church programing guide churches in planning and programing their work locally and also that which they do through associations, state conventions, and the Southern Baptist Convention. This concept of programing magnifies each church and strengthens it for the ministry of Christ.

CHAPTER 4

I. THE TASKS OF THE CONGREGATION
   1. Responsibility to Be a New Testament Church
   2. Responsibility to Participate
   3. Responsibility to Govern
   4. Responsibility to Determine Its Course
   5. Responsibility to Provide Resources
   6. Responsibility to Select Leaders

II. THE TASKS OF THE PASTOR AND THE CHURCH STAFF
   1. Perform Pastoral Responsibilities
   2. Lead the Church to Perform Its Functions

III. THE TASK OF THE DEACONS

IV. THE TASKS OF THE CHURCH COUNCIL

4

The Tasks of the Congregation
and Church Leaders

UNDERSTANDING the nature, purpose, and functions of a church is the beginning point as a church organizes itself for work. With this knowledge for a basis, a church determines the tasks necessary to carry out its work. When it learns the tasks to be done, it organizes to perform them. Church organization is the way members relate themselves to one another in doing specific church tasks.

The initial step as a church organizes tasks is to determine those tasks which because of their nature must be performed by the congregation as a whole. Until it has identified these tasks which the congregation should do and stated its intention with regard to them, it is not ready to assign its other tasks or to bring organizations into being.

The tasks a congregation may assume will depend, of course, on many factors—size, location, leadership, and financial resources. The following, however, seem to be tasks every congregation must assume and must be educated to carry out as a body if it is to be truly a congregational church.

I. THE TASKS OF THE CONGREGATION

1. Responsibility to Be a New Testament Church

Churches cannot attain the purpose Christ set forth, but they can press toward the mark. Striving toward this purpose is the surest evidence that a church is seeking to be a better church. Every congregation should evaluate itself under the leadership of the Holy Spirit. A congregation should seek answers to these questions: Are we the children of God? Are we a fellowship of love? Are we the body of Christ? The answers will give direction to the congregation in its efforts to become the church it was meant to be. Such answers require the leadership of the Holy Spirit and demand time for searching on the part of church members.

2. *Responsibility to Participate*

A church should not neglect to worship, proclaim, educate, and minister. These functions are not just the responsibilities of individuals; they are the actions of the entire body. Many members of Baptist churches "hold membership in" rather than "belong to" the church. Some persons feel that they have the right to decide what they will do and what they will not do. No one should deny the right of any individual to interpret the will of God for his own life. Nor should any child of God who understands his relationship to the body of Christ deny the claim which the church has on him and on each member.

Many activities carried on by churches today are good, and they contribute to its own welfare. They are not, however, necessarily essential to its nature. Many activities are planned to meet the needs of only a part of the membership. Whatever else it does, the congregation as a whole must worship, proclaim, educate, and minister.

This concept of congregational responsibility requires a congregation to take a careful look at the way in which its functions are performed. There is more than one way for an action to be carried out. A method used a few years ago may now have become obsolete and ineffective. As a church grows, it may need to change its ways of doing things. The church must plan its life and work to reflect the uniqueness and individuality of its congregation. The problems of individual members, families, and the congregation need to be reviewed. On the basis of this information, the church should plan its life and work. Having done so, a congregation has a right to expect all members to participate in basic functions of the church.

3. *Responsibility to Govern*

Congregational government, based on the doctrine of the priesthood of the believer, has been a distinctive practice of Baptist churches. Such government has the primary objective of directing affairs of the church for the best spiritual interests of individual members together with the membership as a whole.

True congregational government has often suffered as some Baptist churches have grown too large for the congregations to make all decisions regarding the work of the churches. When congregational government is displaced by another form of government, it has usually been the result of drifting rather than voting to change the manner of operation.

Creative action on the part of the congregation is needed to solve this problem, for congregational government requires continual attention to prevent its perversion. Education in the congregational processes of government is an absolute necessity for Baptist church members. That is why the study of Baptist polity must be given continual attention in the learning opportunities provided by the church.

If a church is to maintain the integrity of its congregational government, it must determine its own course of action, provide resources, and select leaders. Having taken these actions, the church must continually evaluate the work it is doing in terms of the objectives it has set.

Every church member is responsible for participating intelligently in the democratic actions of the congregation. Such participation requires members to understand the nature, purpose, and functions of a church, the relationship of a particular action to the objectives of the church, and arguments for or against the action. Each member should prepare himself through worship to do the will of God and to maintain the fellowship of the church.

4. *Responsibility to Determine Its Course*

Since some activity of a church may not be essential, it is imperative that a congregation determine what it is trying to do.

(1) *Determine its objectives.*—A statement of this determination can become the objectives of the church. With a statement of objectives as a point of orientation, the congregation can then decide which actions will contribute most to the achievement of these objectives.

Churches need to set forth their intentions in stewardship, evangelism, missions, and other areas where they expect to be taking action year after year. Just as a church finds unity of spirit in Christ, setting objectives can give unity to a church's actions.

Congregational government can be exciting when it is concerned with weighty matters. Involving all church members in determining what the church will do also educates them for responsibility. Significant learning can take place in properly conducted church business meetings. Spirit-led seeking, intelligent discussion, questioning, and referral of matters for further study in a fellowship of brotherly love should characterize a church as it determines its course through congregational action.

(2) *Determine Its Programs and Services.*—Baptist churches believe that the congregation should determine by majority consent the course of action it will take. The congregation should authorize and establish programs, program services, and administrative services. The Sunday School program is formed, for example, by grouping the five tasks.

The Library Service consists of four tasks which provide resource materials to enrich and aid in teaching or in training church members to perform the church's functions.

One administrative service is the nominating committee which assists the church in providing leaders for the Brotherhood, the Sunday School, and other organizations of the church.

5. *Responsibility to Provide Resources*

Every Baptist church has resources and means for doing its work. The resources of a church include the Holy Spirit; the time, talents, and money of church members; and facilities of the church. God provides the Holy Spirit; the congregation with God's help must provide the others. The congregation must call forth from its members those resources needed to do its work.

The response is Christian stewardship. This kind of stewardship requires a commitment to Christ and to his work. Christian stewardship is the church member's commitment to the body of Christ and its work in the community and around the world. One's commitment to this work involves his time, talents, and money.

No apology should be made for asking people to do the work of the church. Calling people to perform the tasks of the church is a call from self-centeredness. It is an invitation to participate in congregational action.

Poor administration of the resources of the church leads to misunderstanding and dissatisfaction on the part of members. A congregation has a responsibility to see that its human resources are used wisely.

The congregation is equally responsible for providing the financial resources and physical facilities for the work of a church. Giving money, providing buildings, and supplying equipment should be a spiritual experience. A well-planned interpretation of how and why thousands of dollars of the church's money will be used can make budget-pledging a valuable educational experience. When a church considers constructing a new building, months are usually devoted to discovering and sharing the reasons why the building is needed, why it should be a certain size, why it should be constructed of certain materials, and why it should be designed a certain way.

6. *Responsibility to Select Leaders*

Guidance is necessary if a church is to move toward its objectives. Leaders have the responsibility for giving direction and guidance to the work of the church. Choosing persons to lead the congregation is an important action of the church.

The selected person understands the congregational action to mean that he is serving his church. Of course, the congregation likewise establishes the organizations through which leaders work. Each leader must realize that he is ultimately responsible to the congregation and to God for the work he does.

Selection of leaders is not a trivial action. A mistake at this point can be disastrous. Many problems which disrupt fellowship and split churches could be avoided if congregations approached the task of selecting leaders more seriously. The blind attitude that anybody can do anything contradicts the New Testament teachings about the members of the body of Christ as reviewed previously. An eye is not a hand, nor is a hand a foot. One leader is not the same as another leader. One job does not require the same ability and personality that another requires. Congregations should not be a party simply to putting people to work. Selecting leaders is a holy act. Certainly the Antioch church thought so when it set apart Paul and Barnabas to do the work of that church among the Gentiles. So it should be to Baptist churches today.

The practice of annual election of lay church leaders is the normal procedure in most Baptist churches. This action by the congregation should be properly understood as the best time to get the right people in the right places of service. If a church has made error in a choice during the preceding year, it should take steps to correct the situation at this time.

Refusal to reelect is seldom the best way to handle a worker who has not succeeded in his assignment. Annual election should be a time to review with an individual his efforts and to call him to a higher level of service. Christians are often hesitant to evaluate and discuss the weaknesses of another. This evaluation can be a means for Christian growth when done in Christian love and in the proper manner.

Annual election should be a time of recommitment on the part of every worker who is to serve the church for the coming year. It is a time for each to dedicate himself to improving his leadership abilities. It is the time for leaders to take a new look at what the church is trying to do and to lead creatively toward this goal. Congregations should develop a policy of selecting leaders that takes into account the nature and functions of the church and the worth and capability of each person. The policy of acting on the choice of personnel annually should not be interpreted to mean that workers should be chosen for only one year. Workers should commit themselves to a lifetime of devoted service and improve in this service from one year to the next.

A church must also select its ministers and other employed leaders. This requires special skill. A representative group is not the only criterion to be considered in establishing a pulpit or personnel committee. The question is not whether the prospective worker will please youth or adults. The question is whether this person can fulfil the responsibilities of the job to which the church is calling him. The committee members need to understand the nature of their church, the real desires of the congregation, and the problems which will confront a person who is called as pastor or employee of the church.

Selection of a pastor, minister of education, or minister of music by the congregation should include a commitment by the congregation to grant these persons freedom to work under the direction of the Holy Spirit. A church that is unwilling to grant this freedom has no right to call a minister to leave a pastorate and become their servant in Christ.

II. THE TASKS OF THE PASTOR AND THE CHURCH STAFF

The pastor has two tasks for which he is responsible for performing himself. These major tasks are: (1) perform pastoral responsibilities, and (2) lead the church to perform its functions. These could be divided as shown on page 32.

1. *Perform Pastoral Responsibilities*

The pastor is a proclaimer of the gospel. The congregation expects the pastor to exercise his gift of preaching. They expect him to preach with authority the Word of God to the congregation in a manner that will bring salvation to the lost and will challenge believers to spiritual growth.

A congregation likes to share the preaching of their pastor with the whole community. If he is preaching the Word of God effectively, church members will tell others and will invite them to hear him. The community in which a church is located expects the pastor to preach the Word of God, and they respect him for his work.

The pastor is a leader of worship. He is responsible for conducting corporate worship services, encouraging family and individual worship experiences, and administering the ordinances.

Leading others in the worship of God has been a historic role of the minister. A minister has the heavy responsibility of leading persons to lift their hearts in adoration of God. A Christian worship experience focuses in what God has done for man in Jesus Christ. Responsibilities and opportunities abound for the pastor who leads his people in meaningful worship of God.

A pastor is an educator. He seeks to educate persons in the knowledge and acceptance of Jesus Christ as Saviour and Lord, to train them in the performance of their Christian responsibilities, and to motivate them in Christian living and service.

A pastor also performs acts of ministry as he seeks to meet the needs of persons in Jesus' name. Much of his time goes to pastoral counseling, visiting, performing weddings, conducting funerals, and doing acts of benevolence.

A pastor best reflects Jesus Christ when he is ministering to persons at a time of special need. His presence in time of birth, sickness, or death allows him to share the deepest emotions of the members of his congregation. No other person in a church has this privilege. Such a ministry creates a bond between the pastor and the congregation—a bond of love, of understanding, and of Christian fellowship. Out of such occasions is built the relationship which permits the pastor to counsel with a church member who has personal problems, to exhort the wayward member, and to admonish those who are slow to love. Without this ministry, it is impossible for the pastor to fulfil his total responsibility.

2. *Lead the Church to Perform Its Functions*

Administration is directing people to achieve a goal that is commonly agreed on. It is the process of uniting the efforts of people so that a desired objective is achieved. The basic meaning of "administration" is theological. It means "to minister." The ministry of administration is to direct people to achieve spiritual goals. Administration in a Baptist church is more than just directing or uniting the efforts of people. Administration is a ministry to the total personalities of those being directed or united. The Christian administrator has the responsibility of leading people to use their energies and abilities to achieve the best for their lives. He must seek diligently to aid persons to reach their highest levels of performance. He must lead the ten-talent man to be a ten-talent man and at the same time assure the one-talent man that his efforts also are necessary and valuable. The true administrator is always calling—calling God's people to become what God intends them to be.

As chief administrator of the congregation, the pastor is responsible for overall actions and results in the work of the church. In fulfilling this responsibility, the pastor leads the church to worship, proclaim, educate, and minister. He tries to lead all members of the body to share the common objectives and goals of the congregation. A pastor's administrative responsibility is to lead persons away from the things of the world and into the high calling of Christ Jesus in serving the world.

This responsibility of the pastor demands that he have a clear understanding of the nature, purpose, and functions of a Baptist church. Also he needs skill in planning, overseeing, and evaluating the efforts of the church. He should have the ability to decide on the best course of action.

A pastor needs to understand and to practice the art of delegating responsibility. The wise pastor is one who shares church activities and responsibilities with others. In so doing, he not only extends his own work and accomplishes more but also involves many other persons in the life and work of the church. Some pastors have learned the joy that comes from sharing with others the menial as well as the major tasks in the kingdom of Christ. Such administrative action may require more time, more skill, and more effort, but it strengthens the work of the church.

Some churches have grown so large that more than one minister is needed. In such cases the pastor must serve as the leader of other staff members. The work of such ministers or staff members consists of responsibilities that originally belonged to the pastor. The work of the laity should not be assigned to an employed staff member. To do so will in time weaken the congregational church. Staff members who share the work of the pastor should try to multiply the efforts of the church members through leading them to more effective service.

There are many tasks a pastor can share with others. For instance, the minister of education or the minister of music helps the pastor get his tasks done by leading the program of education or music. These colaborers free the pastor for other service to the church. Having these helpers does not, however, give the pastor more time. It is a well-known fact that supervising other people requires time. The pastor is responsible for leading these persons to minister to the congregation. They, too, must understand the objectives and programs of the congregation. They must understand how their ministry and the programs they lead contribute to the total work of the church. The pastor and staff members must evaluate work that is done to be sure that it is harmonious with the objectives of the church. The pastor must teach church staff members how to use their offices in a spiritual manner.

III. The Task of the Deacons

The office of deacon had its beginning in the days of the apostles. Finding themselves overburdened with everyday matters while seeking to preach the gospel, to administer the functions of the body of Christ, and to minister to the members, the apostles asked the church for assistance. The first helpers waited on tables and made decisions regarding the distribution of food. Just as the office was established to assist the apostles, deacons in Baptist churches today are chosen to assist the pastor in doing his work. They should support his ministry.

Deacons are not the rulers of the church. Rather, they are called to minister. The word "deacon" is derived from the

Greek word *diakonia,* which originally meant one who waits on tables. The word *diakonos* came to mean "servant" in the New Testament church. Performing personal ministries to all the members of a congregation is a major task for many pastors. The larger the congregation, the more difficult the task. Pastors and deacons need to share responsibility in this work. They have as their primary responsibility the welfare of church members. Scriptural qualifications for deacons demand that they be men of the highest spiritual and moral quality. This requirement is necessary if they are to perform the spiritual ministry of their office. Deacons should be the most prayerful and the most deeply concerned group in a church.

Simply stated, the task of the deacon is to assist the pastor to perform the pastoral ministry. For further clarification this task might be broken into the following more precise aspects.

1. Assist pastor in conducting corporate worship
2. Assist pastor in encouraging family worship
3. Assist pastor in administering ordinances
4. Assist pastor in the preaching program
5. Assist pastor in witnessing
6. Assist pastor in performing pastoral counseling
7. Assist pastor in performing pastoral visitation
8. Assist pastor in performing acts of benevolence
9. Assist pastor in building and maintaining Christian fellowship
10. Assist pastor in interpreting the program of the church

IV. THE TASKS OF THE CHURCH COUNCIL

A congregation assigns certain of its responsibilities to the church council for performance. In doing this, the congregation is not abdicating the ultimate responsibility for the tasks. The congregation does look, however, to the church council to supply certain staff services, of an advisory and informative nature, on which the congregation can make its decisions.

The church council is an advisory and correlating agency through which all organizations and committees may coordinate their activities into one harmonious program of work. It is not an authoritative or administrative group. Once it agrees on a program or project, the head of one of the church organizations or the chairman of a church committee becomes responsible for carrying out the program or project.

The primary tasks a church might assign to the church council are:

1. Formulate and recommend to the congregation suggested church objectives and goals
2. Develop and recommend to the congregation strategies for reaching church goals
3. Review and coordinate suggested program plans and actions of church officers, organizations, and committees; and provide for adequate communication among church officers, organizations, and committees
4. Review and report as appropriate to the congregation the use of resources in terms of the needs of church programs as they work toward the achievement of the objectives and goals of a church
5. Evaluate program achievements in terms of church objectives and goals and report evaluations to the congregation

The church council assists the congregation by coordinating suggested actions to secure maximum effort, and by making suggestions to prevent overlapping in program plans before they are recommended to the congregation.

In fulfilling its assignment, a church council should be careful not to violate the direct reporting relationships of the various church organizations and committees to the congregation. When the church council reviews program plans and coordinates suggested program actions of church officers and organizations, the coordinated plans are recommended by the appropriate program leaders to the congregation. After discussion in the council, any organizational leader who disagrees with decisions there is free to request the congregation to hear his views before it makes its decision.

CHAPTER 5

I. TEACH THE BIBLICAL REVELATION
  1. Nature of the Biblical Revelation
  2. Content of the Biblical Revelation
  3. Purpose of the Biblical Revelation

II. LEAD IN REACHING ALL PROSPECTS FOR THE CHURCH
  1. The Meaning of "Lead In"
  2. The Meaning of "Reaching" and "Prospects"

III. LEAD ALL CHURCH MEMBERS TO WORSHIP, WITNESS, LEARN, AND MINISTER DAILY
  1. Man's Need and Capacity for Worship
  2. Christ's Command to Witness
  3. Christians As Learners
  4. Ministering in Jesus' Name
  5. Relationship with Training Union

IV. PROVIDE ORGANIZATION AND LEADERSHIP FOR SPECIAL PROJECTS OF THE CHURCH
  1. Preparation for, and Participation in, Revival Meetings
  2. Subscribing the Church Budget
  3. Sharing in Promotion of Missions Offerings

V. PROVIDE AND INTERPRET INFORMATION REGARDING THE WORK OF THE CHURCH AND THE DENOMINATION

5

The Sunday School Program
of a Church

EDUCATION is one of the functions of a church. Involving church members in learning is so necessary that a church cannot be a church in its fullest sense if it fails to educate its members. Many Southern Baptist churches give strong emphasis to their function of education. They have developed educational programs according to the pattern defined in chapter 3. These churches have entrusted to these programs much of the responsibility for educating their constituencies. (For clearer understanding of this chapter, consult Glossary for the meaning of "program.")

In addition, Southern Baptist churches expect their program organizations to perform major tasks which are related to their educational responsibilities. This assignment gives each program significant church tasks to perform and properly relates the program to the work of the churches.

In this chapter and in subsequent ones, the tasks of the various church program organizations will be discussed. In each instance the study portion (content area) and the related tasks of the program will be considered.

The program organization carrying the heaviest responsibilities is the Sunday School. It is ideally suited for this position of trust. The textbook of the Sunday School is the Bible, which is foundational to all other study tasks of the church program organizations. Most Southern Baptist churches have Sunday Schools, and their combined enrolment is the largest Sunday School membership in the world. The Sunday School is a permanent program meeting each Sunday and conducting its work regularly each week. It involves the largest number of workers.

Vacation Bible School and Weekday Bible Study are special expressions of a Sunday School. This work enhances and enlarges the Sunday School program of a church.

Consideration of a church's organized programs should begin with a study of the principal tasks of the Sunday School.

I. TEACH THE BIBLICAL REVELATION

The Bible has been the textbook of the Sunday School from the development of the first lesson courses to the present. But there are many ways to study the Bible. For example, one might begin with Genesis and study the Bible book by book, a chapter a Sunday. But if Bible study were conducted according to this pattern, a child would reach voting age before beginning his study of Matthew.

The most effective approach to Bible study is through teaching the biblical revelation. This means teaching the Bible in terms of the revelation it records concerning God and his will for men. "Revelation in the Christian sense is that self-disclosure of God in Christ which makes it possible for man to know God and to live a life of fellowship with him. . . . The record of this revelation—the literary means of its transmission to us—is the Bible" (W. T. Conner, *Christian Doctrine*). For these reasons we refer to the Sunday School's content area as the biblical revelation.

Reaching persons for Bible study is a basic task of the Sunday School. Teaching requires that there be someone to learn. A teaching situation consists of *something to teach, a teacher, a learner,* and *effective communication between the two*. In Christian teaching we have, in addition, the essential work of the Holy Spirit.

As scriptural authority for reaching people, we often quote Luke 14:23: "The lord said unto the servant, Go out into the highways and hedges, and compel them to come in, that my house may be filled." Unfortunately, we do this without studying the preceding verses. The marriage feast had already been prepared, and the guests who were invited failed to come. For that reason the servants were told to find other guests. *Reach-*

*ing individuals is the responsibility of every Sunday School;
but when we reach these individuals, we are obligated to provide adequate Bible study for them.* Before going after prospects, a Sunday School should make certain that every person
invited to attend will be spiritually fed when he comes.

The importance of the content to be learned provides the
reason for reaching people who will study it. Therefore, we
start the discussion of the tasks of the Sunday School with a
consideration of what the Sunday School is to teach. For years
emphasis in the Sunday School has been on the study of the
Bible. It is the value and importance of the content of the
Bible which should motivate each Sunday School worker to
reach people for Bible study.

Since what is to be studied in the Sunday School is so
important, let us examine further what is meant by the biblical
revelation.

1. *Nature of the Biblical Revelation*

The biblical revelation is God's disclosure of himself and
his will for man as recorded in the Bible. Since the beginning
of man's existence, God has sought to reveal himself to man.
These revelations came in creation and in God's dealing with
men individually and collectively through a long period of
history. The biblical revelation brings to man the most important and vital facts about God. Thus it is supremely our source
of truth about God.

God had to work by degrees in revealing himself to men.
In the early stages of men's experience with God, they were
not ready for his full revelation. For this reason, the New
Testament phase of the revelation stands on higher spiritual
and moral ground than does the Old. The Old Testament is
fully understood only in the light of the New; similarly, a proper
understanding of the Old Testament is necessary in rightly interpreting the New.

The theme of both Old and New Testaments is the redemption of sinful man. This is the theme which unifies the Bible
in its record of the revelation of God in his seeking love.

Both divine and human factors were involved as God

breathed on men to bring into being the inspired writings. He directed the selection of the books through the general consensus of spiritually discerning believers, and he guided in the preservation of these inspired books down to the present day.

2. *Content of the Biblical Revelation*

In the biblical revelation we see God in his relationships to man, to his created universe, and to history. We see man as he was created (in the image of God), as he now is in his broken relationship with God through pride and disobedience (a sinner), and as he can become in redemption (a child of God, a new creation). We see the supreme revelation of God through his Son, reconciling sinful man to God and breaking down the barriers between man and man.

The life, death, and resurrection of Christ were the climax of God's self-disclosure, but by no means the conclusion of it. The marvelous activity of the Holy Spirit in the life and work of the church was necessary to demonstrate and interpret the full meaning of God's revelation through Christ.

The church is the fellowship of believers under the lordship of Jesus Christ and led by the Holy Spirit. The nature, purpose, and functions of the church progressively unfold in the New Testament writings.

God included in his self-disclosure the person and work of the Holy Spirit. Although the nature and work of the Spirit may be seen throughout the Old Testament, it is only in the New Testament that his person and ministry are fully revealed. The Spirit came in power at Pentecost. He works in and through the church to convict men of sin, to interpret the revelation of God in Christ, and to be the personal guide and enabling power in the life of every believer.

In God's self-disclosure we see him ruling over the universe and the affairs of men. Although this rule is now limited by man's freedom of will and consequent rebellion, God will in the end be triumphant. He will judge men and history, and the universe will be completely submissive to his will. In this consummation of the kingdom, the redemption of man and of the created universe will be complete. Redeemed men will be liberated from the limitations of earthly existence in the complete freedom of fellowship with, and service to, God.

3. *Purpose of the Biblical Revelation*

The purpose of the biblical revelation is to bring men face to face with God in Christ and to confront them with the necessity of responding to him with trusting love and obedience. This response brings men into a living relationship with God within which they can fulfil God's unique and creative purpose for them.

The Sunday School has been entrusted with teaching this record of God's self-disclosure. This involves teaching not only the content of the Bible but also its meaning, value, and relevance to the lives of learners. The purpose of teaching the biblical revelation is to bring learners to personal commitment to Jesus Christ as Lord and Saviour, and to growth toward spiritual maturity and Christlikeness. Such teaching also leads churches to understand, accept, and assume their responsibility for making known to the world God's self-disclosure and for guiding men to Jesus Christ.

Understanding these purposes gives meaning not only to the Sunday School task of teaching the biblical revelation but also to its task of outreach.

II. LEAD IN REACHING ALL PROSPECTS FOR THE CHURCH

Jesus said, "As my Father hath sent me, even so send I you" (John 20:21). He also said to his disciples, "Pray ye therefore the Lord of the harvest, that he will send forth labourers into his harvest" (Matt. 9:38). As a final commission to his followers, Jesus said, "Go ye therefore, and teach all nations, baptizing them in the name of the Father, and of the Son, and of the Holy Ghost" (Matt. 28:19). These and many other commands of Jesus indicate that a church ought always to have compassion and concern for those not being reached.

Concern for the unreached is one of the basic characteristics of a church. If a church does not have this concern, is it a church? Every church must be concerned about the members already enlisted—whether they are growing, developing, and maturing as church members. But if a church becomes wholly introspective, it tends to become self-centered and self-satisfied. The result is a dying church.

What is happening today? Many church members are neglecting to share the expression of their church's concern for all men. Some members of almost every church are looking for an excuse to stop church growth. They even talk of buying the last piece of property and constructing the last building. They often take this attitude in the midst of unlimited prospects at their doors and with millions of lost people in distant lands.

The reluctance of many Christians to meet their responsibilities in outreach, in keeping with Christ's commission, calls for positive and immediate action. Southern Baptist churches must clarify and make definite assignment of the task of leading in reaching all prospects for the church. History, logic, and past experience indicate the use of the Sunday School as the strategic approach to a church's continuing outreach.

The assignment of this task to the Sunday School is appropriate for a number of reasons. First, the teaching of the biblical revelation helps stimulate proper motivation for seeking to bring persons to a full relationship with Christ and his church. The assignment of this task for the Sunday School is also appropriate because of the scope of the task. All Christians have a responsibility in outreach. More people belong to the Sunday School than to any other church organization, and almost all of those enrolled in other organizations are also in Sunday School. A church can more readily involve all its members in outreach through its Sunday School than in any other way.

Another reason for assigning this task of outreach to the Sunday School is that it is more likely to enrol evangelistic prospects than other organizations. Although there are exceptions, an unsaved or unaffiliated person is usually more easily reached for Sunday School than for other organizations. The Sunday School is the church organization specifically designed to include the unsaved and the unaffiliated.

1. *The Meaning of "Lead In"*

From a practical standpoint, the major responsibility for reaching all prospects for a church must be accepted by the Sunday School. This means that a church would look to the Sunday School to determine and evaluate outreach opportunities open to the church. *Specifically the Sunday School should plan and conduct a balanced and coordinated plan of outreach. This plan should appropriately involve all program organizations. Such a plan should include and implement necessary Sunday School actions designed to reach all prospects.*

Other church program organizations have a supporting role in reaching prospects for the church. Their efforts should always be properly related to the Sunday School's plan.

For instance, the Sunday School might propose some missions actions. These actions would become a church's organized effort to extend its ministry to persons of special need or circumstance; to those who are not presently enrolled in the Sunday School or are not prospects for membership in the church or its program.

The Woman's Missionary Union and the Brotherhood support the task of reaching prospects for the church as they carry out special missions actions. Woman's Missionary Union and Brotherhood may establish mission Sunday Schools, conduct Vacation Bible Schools in migrant camps or underprivileged areas, or conduct Bible classes in rest homes or in other institutions.

Through involving church members in its study of the biblical concept of outreach, the Sunday School keeps before all persons the importance of reaching all prospects. The Sunday School has responsibility for involving church members in the overall visitation program of a church.

In addition, the Sunday School carries out specific actions in its own work of reaching all prospects for the church. It seeks to enrol in Sunday School all prospects for the church. It has responsibility for establishing branch Sunday Schools, Extension Bible classes, and branch Vacation Bible Schools where these are planned as a means for starting a church, or to gain new members for the existing church.

The Training Union provides the necessary training for the development of skills in outreach. It also has a vital part in the task of reaching all prospects through its responsibility for properly orienting new church members, thus helping to involve them effectively in the life of a church.

The Music Ministry makes its definite contribution to reaching all prospects by making more attractive and meaningful the regular services of worship, offering participation in choirs and music activities, and contributing to the use of effective music in the various organizations of a church.

2. *The Meaning of "Reaching" and "Prospects"*

The task of reaching all prospects is essentially the work that a church does in issuing a continuous invitation to persons to share in everything a church has to offer. Reaching prospects requires maintaining personal contact with every unsaved and unenrolled person in the community in order to establish a relationship with him for Christ and the church. The ultimate purpose of outreach is to bring each prospect under the influence of the gospel. A means of accomplishing this purpose is by leading the prospect to participate in the educational organizations and the worship services of the church.

If the outreach purpose is reached, each unsaved person will be won to Christ and will be led to place his membership in a church, to participate in the programs of the church educational organizations, and to engage in Christian service as a faithful church member.

Reaching out to enrol all unenlisted persons for Bible study is basic if persons are to be reached permanently for Christ and the church. If the prospects can attend, they should be enrolled in the departments which meet on Sunday. If, because of work or health, prospects cannot attend regularly, they should be enrolled in a weektime department or the Extension department, or be provided for in a class-related ministry. In this way, these prospects may be visited regularly and given individual guidance in Bible study. The Nursery ministry likewise provides an outreach to children under four and their parents.

However, reaching all prospects means more than enrolling and teaching individuals in classes. Reaching, in the sense used here, means that each prospect is being visited regularly for the church by some member of the Sunday School. Although the Sunday School member desires the prospect to be in Sunday School and is working to that end, his main purpose is to meet the personal needs of the prospect until he is led to attend and participate.

Teaching in this case may be done in homes and places of business according to the informal teaching opportunities which develop during visits. Such teaching can be done best through conversation in which Scripture passages appropriate to the needs and problems of each person are used at the most opportune time. Through regular visitation each prospect can be kept in touch with the church. In some cases such personal contacts may need to be maintained over the years, even though a person never attends on Sunday.

The Sunday School's role, then, in leading in reaching all prospects for the church involves providing an overall plan for outreach in which other church program organizations find an appropriate place, conducting a continuing visitation program for the church, and enrolling all available prospects in the Sunday School.

III. Lead All Church Members to Worship, Witness, Learn, and Minister Daily

The study of the biblical revelation should result in Christian growth. Growth will be manifested in daily living as the Christian worships, witnesses, learns, and ministers daily.

1. *Man's Need and Capacity for Worship*

God created man with the need and capacity for worship. He provided for this need to be met and this capacity to be exercised in daily fellowship with him. Before man can have fellowship with God through worship, however, he must first know God. His desire to worship will grow and his practice of worship will develop as this knowledge increases. The Sunday School can stimulate and guide the practice of worship by helping persons grow in knowledge of God and by providing opportunities for personal encounter with God.

Attendance at a worship service should never be equated with genuine worship. Corporate worship opportunities are essential in the life of a church. These experiences provide one of the most effective means of helping Christians become aware of God's presence and to respond to him in trusting love and obedience.

One way a Sunday School contributes effectively to the corporate worship in a church is by leading members to attend. A visit to reach people should include an invitation to attend the church worship services. When a member or visitor attends Sunday School, he should be invited to remain for the morning worship service.

Not only should the Sunday School lead members to attend the church worship services; it should plan for worship experiences in Sunday School and Vacation Bible School. Assembly programs and Vacation Bible Schools offer excellent opportunities for worship. If properly prepared, these programs can provide the atmosphere, suitable materials, and dedicated leadership conducive to genuine worship.

However, the Sunday School's greatest opportunity to lead church members to worship comes within the fellowship of the class. As class members and teacher study God's Word together, there should be a consciousness of God's presence. Bible study should lead to quiet moments which cause persons to respond to the admonition: "Be still, and know that I am God." A major purpose of teachers should be to provide experiences which will lead their pupils to respond to God in loving obedience. The teacher can become aware of the class member's need for growth in worship in a way impossible for a pastor in a worship service.

The teacher will not only lead his pupils to experience worship in the class but also help them to carry such experiences into daily living. Both individual and family worship are vital;

they are daily, continuing needs for the Christian. Prayer, biblical material outlined in lesson courses, and devotional reading are important elements of individual and family worship.

As a part of its church-assigned task of leading members to worship, the Sunday School will work with the Training Union, Music Ministry, Woman's Missionary Union, and Brotherhood in leading all church members to attend the Sunday evening and midweek prayer services of their churches. These additional worship opportunities are neglected by many church members. As the Sunday School lends this support to the Sunday evening services of the church, it will lead increasing numbers of church members to use Sunday evening for fellowship with God.

As the Sunday School leads each church member to worship daily, the Training Union trains church members in the art of worship. Special materials are provided for this purpose, so that the Sunday School and the Training Union work together in making worship central in the experiences of church members.

2. *Christ's Command to Witness*

(1) *Meaning of witness.*—To witness is to share with others one's experience in Christ. "Witness" is a term used by Jesus: "But ye shall receive power, after that the Holy Ghost is come upon you: and ye shall be witnesses unto me both in Jerusalem, and in all Judaea, and in Samaria, and unto the uttermost part of the earth" (Acts 1:8). Christians are compelled by the commission of Christ to share with others what God through Christ has done for them. This witness should be given to the unsaved persons with whom one has contact. Every church member should be constantly alert to opportunities to express to such persons what God through Christ means to him.

Christians also should witness to one another. Christians are encouraged as they bear to one another a testimony regarding the blessings of God which they have experienced. In the church prayer meeting of another generation, this kind of witnessing was done regularly. In recent years, little opportunity has been afforded for this type of spiritual experience in church life. (This lack may explain in part the various types of prayer retreats and cell groups which are becoming increasingly popular.) When church members share their spiritual experiences with one another, their faith is strengthened. Such conversation is needed as Christian friends talk together.

By giving money through the church budget, Christians can provide a witness through those who serve as missionaries. Although such indirect witnessing can in no wise take the place of personal witnessing, it is vastly important. Christ's command included not only "Jerusalem" but also "the ends of the earth."

(2) *Witnessing, the responsibility of every Christian.*—Perhaps a large group of church members feel that witnessing is the responsibility of the pastor, the employed staff of the church, the deacons, and the Sunday School officers and teachers. When these workers were selected, the church members who approved them happily voted for them to do the evangelistic work of the church.

Such concepts cannot be justified by the New Testament. Witnessing is the responsibility of every Christian. Until a church deliberately sets itself to lead the members of the church to witness, it is falling short of the biblical concept of a New Testament church.

(3) *Taking advantage of witnessing opportunities.*—The Christian must learn to recognize and take advantage of opportunities to witness daily. Early Christians were led to say, "We cannot but speak the things which we have seen and heard" (Acts 4:20). There was such joy in their hearts over the wonderful things God had done for them that they could not refrain from telling others. Contemporary Christians should be having experiences with the Lord and should be sharing these experiences with their associates.

Can one witness without speaking? Certainly the life of the Christian strengthens or weakens the words which he speaks. One's attitude when he wakes in the morning, the way he drives his car, his manner of speaking to his family and business associates, as well as his choices of recreation, relate to his witness. One may not assume that the courteous driver is a

Christian, but questions arise concerning the reckless driver who one knows is a professing Christian. Christians must be so filled with the Spirit that their actions support their spoken testimony.

The Christian who is unresponsive to his witnessing obligation may confront and reject many witnessing opportunities in one day. This same Christian may go at night to engage in his church's planned visitation, but he may contact fewer prospects than he could have encountered all day at his work. Many churches worry about their "territory." There is a simple answer to this dilemma. In witnessing, a church's territory may be defined by the activities of its members.

We must practice the New Testament concept that witnessing begins when we awaken in the morning and continues throughout our waking hours. We should be sensitive and alert to every opportunity to witness for Christ, whether to the saved or the unsaved. A positive Christian testimony is needed in every area of life. When we seriously accept this responsibility, Christianity will become the world force Christ intended it to be.

(4) *Sunday School, the logical organization for leading church members to witness.*—The Sunday School, through its program of teaching the biblical revelation, helps stimulate motivation for Christian witnessing. As God speaks to Christians through his Word, they find both the mandate and the message for witnessing.

Sunday School classes provide excellent opportunities for witnessing. The relaxed, informal atmosphere of a small group engaged in Bible study encourages the sharing of experiences. Through its program of outreach, the Sunday School has contact with many persons, saved and unsaved, who need some Christian's witness.

Through its organization, the Sunday School has the means to assign responsibility for witnessing to every person whom the church should reach. A warm and favorable witnessing climate is provided when prospects are associated with Sunday School workers and Christian class members. Such informal contacts also provide favorable circumstances for Christian-to-

Christian witnessing. The enlistment of every church member in witnessing can become the church's thrust into the surrounding unregenerate community.

3. *Christians As Learners*

In the New Testament, Christians were considered disciples, or learners. The church has been described as a fellowship of learners. The Sunday School has the task of leading members to become learners in the New Testament sense.

Jesus said, "Take my yoke upon you, and learn from me" (Matt. 11:29, RSV). Followers of Jesus are to do more than learn *about* him; they are to learn from personal relationship with him in all areas of life. He said, "I am the way, the truth, and the life: no man cometh unto the Father, but by me" (John 14:6).

Man is by nature a learner. He is not a passive being, responding only to the forces in his environment. He is a living being with motives of the heart and mental and physical drives which result in intellectual curiosity. A vital relationship with Christ is the most effective motivation of learning. The Christian should be highly motivated to learn from his relationship with Christ, and to learn from all sources whatever will help him serve Christ better.

Although the desire to learn is present in all persons in varying degrees, it must be stimulated. Many think of learning as a task to be completed by the end of the school years and avoided in the future. Some persons may see the educational organizations of the church as opportunities to demonstrate loyalty to the church rather than as opportunities for learning. The Sunday School has the responsibility of kindling intellectual fires and leading members to become enthusiastic learners.

Learning must not be equated with membership in an organization. The desire for learning may—and often should—result in participation in organized learning situations; but such participation must be viewed as a means rather than an end. The church has a responsibility for providing resources for learning, but the desire for learning must motivate use of these resources.

Any learning which will enrich the church member's relationship with Christ or increase the effectiveness of his Christian service falls within the scope of the task: lead all church members to learn daily. Appropriate learnings may involve individual study or participation in learning opportunities sponsored by the Sunday School or other church organizations, or in some instances by other groups. For instance, nonreaders might be led to participate in a literacy class. A unit in the Sunday School curriculum related to the mission of a church might result in studies of contemporary missions in Woman's Missionary Union or Brotherhood. A Primary Sunday School teacher might enrol in elementary education classes in a college or university. A Young People's teacher might study counseling.

As Sunday School teachers and pupils study the Bible together, teachers will be alert for opportunities to stimulate within each pupil a desire to "study to shew . . . [himself] approved unto God."

4. *Ministering in Jesus' Name*

The Sunday School has the task of leading all church members to minister daily. This means involving members in a continuing response in Jesus' name to the needs of persons.

(1) *The need for ministering.*—The needs of persons are varied and changing. Such needs may be spiritual, physical, emotional, mental, and social. Special needs of persons may exist because of the sinful nature of man, weaknesses at birth, developmental conditions, tensions in life, wrong actions in judgment of persons, inadequate education and training, influences from society, accidents, and inadequate employment.

When life was much less complex and conditions encouraged more interdependence, neighbors seemed more concerned with one another's problems. Farmers gathered to rebuild a burned barn or to harvest the crops of the neighbor who was ill. Sitting up with sick friends was common. People took time to demonstrate their concern.

In today's complex society, however, one may not know the person who lives next door. Like the priest and the Levite, we pass by on the other side. We do not want to become involved.

In almost every community we find those who are in need of food, clothing, and shelter. There are those who are lonely. Such persons are found in rest homes, in hospitals, in jails, in homes for unwed mothers, in juvenile detention homes, in orphanages, and even in our churches. The person in need of a friend is not necessarily confined to lower economic and social groups. The divorcée in the fashionable apartment, the international student in the college dormitory, the alcoholic in the gutter, and the widow who is suddenly left alone have at least one thing in common: each is in need of someone who will put into practice in its deepest meaning a verse learned in childhood, "Be ye kind one to another, tenderhearted, forgiving one another, even as God for Christ's sake hath forgiven you" (Eph. 4:32).

(2) *Christ, the example.*—The ministry of Christ abounds with examples of his concern for the physical, mental, social, and spiritual needs of persons. He forgave sinners, healed lepers, gave sight to the blind, cast out demons, and raised Lazarus from the dead.

One of the best condensed statements of Christ's concern for the physical needs of persons is found in Matthew 25:35-36: "For I was an hungred and ye gave me meat: I was thirsty, and ye gave me drink: I was a stranger, and ye took me in: naked, and ye clothed me: I was sick, and ye visited me: I was in prison, and ye came unto me." In ministering to personal needs of persons, one ministers to Christ.

(3) *Sunday School members, the responsible persons.*— Through outreach and witnessing, church members will discover many persons with varying needs. Christians should endeavor to meet these needs in the spirit of Christ. Such persons need someone to understand them, love them, and express compassion and concern for them. Some are members of a church; others are not. The church exists to meet the needs of all persons.

There are civic agencies which attempt to meet many community needs. A church is not to compete with such agencies.

In some instances, the most effective help may be referral to the appropriate community resources. Christian ministering may include, but goes far beyond, furnishing a hot meal, a wheelchair, or a Thanksgiving basket. Christian ministering involves sharing Christian love.

5. *Relationship with Training Union*

In the task of leading church members to worship, witness, learn, and minister, the Sunday School has a close relationship with the Training Union. The Sunday School is to make the members aware of the need for the performance of these functions. The Sunday School has the responsibility of providing the motivation, opportunity, and guidance in performing the functions.

The Training Union is given the responsibility of training the members to perform the functions. The Sunday School's task of "leading" depends heavily on the church member's being trained for the work he is being led to do.

IV. Provide Organization and Leadership for Special Projects of the Church*

Because of the nature, purpose, and functions of the Sunday School, it can be helpful in conducting special projects which are related to its Bible-teaching ministry. Assignment to the Sunday School of certain projects which are in line with its tasks and its constituency can insure the maximum success of the project.

A project is an activity which can be conducted in a brief period of days or weeks. Following are some projects usually assigned to a Sunday School:

1. *Preparation for, and Participation in, Revival Meetings*

The Sunday School is the church's most valuable organized force for use preceding, during, and following revival meetings. The Sunday School may be used to take a census prior to a

---

* The Sunday School shares this task with the other church program organizations. Churches assign different projects to the organizations in line with their basic tasks.

revival meeting and thus provide witnessing opportunities. With the census information in hand, the leaders of the Sunday School can tabulate the names of the evangelistic prospects of the church. These prospects include not only persons found in the census but also unsaved and unchurched Sunday School members. Prospects will include the unsaved and unchurched parents of Sunday School members. Use of the Sunday School witnessing plan in a church has proved valuable in winning the unsaved.

During the revival the Sunday School should lead all church members to witness and to invite prospects to attend the services.

Superintendents and/or pastor may use assembly time to point up the claims of Christ, urging the importance of public profession of faith in Christ. Teachers and class members may bear a strong witness in the class session. Such witnessing will be excellent preparation for revival decision services.

The Sunday School is also helpful in the follow-up of revivals. New converts may be assigned to the Sunday School for visitation and enlistment. The concern of Sunday School workers for the unsaved by no means stops when the convert is baptized. Sunday School officers and teachers should encourage participation in New Church Member Orientation. Continued instruction in the Christian life is effectively provided through studying the biblical revelation. Bible study, the lifelong need of every church member, should be recognized as such not only by the church but also by individual church members.

Sunday School workers should encourage all new church members to enrol in other church organizations and participate in the total life and work of the church. This is another way the Sunday School contributes to the development of the new church member and to the growth of other church organizations.

2. *Subscribing the Church Budget*

The Sunday School has become the church's chief instrument in subscribing church budgets, and it is impossible to teach the biblical revelation without teaching stewardship. Such teaching requires time and must cover the basic principles of stewardship necessary for a person to become a faithful steward of his possessions. A Christian must grow spiritually in order to become a good steward. On the other hand, giving encourages spiritual growth.

The Sunday School is useful in making preparation for a church budget campaign. Opportunity can be provided members to sign pledge cards in their departments or classes. Here a teacher has the advantage of encouraging personal participation because of his contacts with his pupils. A teacher may encourage his class members to sign pledge cards and thereby teach the stewardship of money. Learning should result in practice. Therefore, what a person learns regarding the stewardship of money should be expressed in making a pledge to the church budget.

The Sunday School teacher is also the best person for the task of obtaining pledges from Sunday School members who are absent when pledges are made. Teachers should visit their class members regularly. When this practice is followed, the teacher's visit to obtain a pledge is normal procedure. Sunday School workers can find ways to remind church members of the importance of faithful giving in keeping with pledges made. By providing offering envelopes to be used each Sunday, the Sunday School emphasizes the values of a budget system.

3. *Sharing in Promotion of Missions Offerings*

In 20 percent of Southern Baptist churches, the Sunday School is the only church educational organization. For this reason, the Sunday School is used for missions days and offerings. Home Missions Day in the Sunday School and Foreign Missions Day in the Sunday School now follow the home missions and foreign missions weeks of prayer in the denominational calendar. The Sunday School Department of the Sunday School Board cooperates with the two mission boards, Woman's Missionary Union, and the Brotherhood in presenting annually opportunities for giving financial and prayer support to these two missions causes. Sunday Schools also present state missions, at which time special offerings are received in many states.

Of particular assistance to the churches in evangelism, stewardship, and missions is the Vacation Bible School. It provides one of the most valuable opportunities the church has for winning children and youth to Christ. An increasing number are being won to Christ and are making life commitments during Vacation Bible School. The Vacation Bible School also gives major emphasis to the Cooperative Program. The offerings increase from year to year, but the most valuable contribution is stewardship education. Educating Vacation Bible School pupils in the needs of denominational causes strengthens the future program of Southern Baptist churches.

V. Provide and Interpret Information Regarding the Work of the Church and the Denomination*

One of the responsibilities of the Sunday School is to help the church develop a well-informed, responsive constituency.

A major need in our churches is intelligent involvement of more members in the work of Christ through the churches and the denomination. The complexity of church life today makes communication difficult but imperative if members are to assume their responsibilities.

The nature of the task of providing and interpreting information regarding the work of the church and denomination is primarily educational. Therefore, it is natural that it should be assigned to the educational organizations of the church. In this context it is possible to interpret this information according to the needs and interests of varying constituent groups.

The information to be channeled should be related to the church's functions: worship, proclamation, education, and ministry. Information should also be given regarding the life and work of the church carried on in cooperation with other churches on the associational, state, and Convention levels, and through the Baptist World Alliance. The information to be

---

* The Sunday School shares this task with the other church program organizations.

provided should be significant, in the sense that some measure of judgment should be exercised. This judgment may be made on the basis of the relevance of the information to the church's basic functions, the objectives of this task, and other valid criteria. (The Sunday School is only one of several channels of information and interpretation. One method of judging what to channel through the Sunday School is to study the information in the light of the Sunday School's tasks.) Care must be taken not to make department and class sessions purely promotional in nature. The teaching period should be protected at all costs.

The information and interpretation should be made available to persons of all age groups in line with their age, maturity, and need for the particular information. The Sunday School can disseminate both church and denominational information in such a way as to unify the entire Sunday School program. This will properly relate the Sunday School program to the church and through the church to the denomination. *The Sunday School Builder* and other Sunday School publications carry significant denominational information. This makes it possible for every Sunday School member to know what his denomination is emphasizing month by month.

CHAPTER 6

I. TEACH MISSIONS

   1. The Content of Missions

   2. The Importance of Teaching Missions

II. LEAD PERSONS TO PARTICIPATE IN MISSIONS

   1. Relationships of Study and Other Actions in Woman's Missionary Union

   2. Areas of Participation in Missions

   3. Missions Actions

III. PROVIDE ORGANIZATION AND LEADERSHIP FOR SPECIAL MISSIONS PROJECTS OF THE CHURCH

   1. The Nature and Purpose of Special Projects

   2. Special Missions Projects Led by Woman's Missionary Union

IV. PROVIDE AND INTERPRET INFORMATION REGARDING THE WORK OF THE CHURCH AND THE DENOMINATION

6

The Woman's Missionary Union Program of a Church

WOMAN'S MISSIONARY UNION is the church's program organization for providing missionary education for children, girls, young women, and adult women. The organizations of WMU are Sunbeam Band for children, Girls' Auxiliary for Junior and Intermediate girls, Young Woman's Auxiliary for young women, and Woman's Missionary Society for adult women. The Brotherhood in a church is the missionary education program organization for boys, young men, and men.

In addition to conducting its ongoing study and action program for its members, Woman's Missionary Union seeks to involve the entire church membership in missions study and missions actions.

The study of missions is significant in the life of the church. The major resources of other church programs are spent in helping the church realize its mission in its immediate area— reaching people for church membership and cultivating the life of the church itself. In contrast, the programs of Woman's Missionary Union and Brotherhood lead the church to awareness of, and response to, the mission of the church beyond itself, to the end of the world. These two organizations keep church members aware that they have responsibilities not only for the people in the community served by the church but also for people of the whole world.

Woman's Missionary Union is third in total membership among the church program organizations. It also ranks third among these organizations in the number of churches in which it functions.

Woman's Missionary Union can perform at least four essential tasks for a church.

I. TEACH MISSIONS

The content area of missions is a part of the total curriculum of a Southern Baptist church. This study area builds on the study of the biblical revelation and relates to the other content areas of the church.

1. *The Content of Missions*

The content area of Woman's Missionary Union consists of the missionary message of the Bible, the progress of Christian missions, and contemporary missions.

(1) *The missionary message of the Bible.*—Missions cannot be understood adequately without understanding the missionary message of the Bible. Therefore, the study of missions in Woman's Missionary Union includes content which reveals God's missionary purpose for all persons. The missionary message of the Bible begins with the Old Testament. Woman's Missionary Union studies God's missionary plan from the Old Testament through the entire Bible.

The Old Testament reveals missions in the plan of God. Man's sin is the reason for missions. Abraham has been referred to as the first missionary. He was chosen as an agent in God's missionary plan. Abraham became a foreign missionary, for he left his own people to live in a country of God's own choice.

The prophets were messengers of world missions. Since their messages are rich in missionary content, the prophets receive attention in the study of missions in the Bible. These messages reveal the universality of the love of God and his desire to bring all nations into a knowledge of his love and purpose. These are but examples of the wealth of missions content in the Old Testament.

The New Testament offers the richest field of study for missions. The coming of Christ, the establishment of his church, and the launching of the Christian missionary enterprise make the New Testament a story of world missions. During Jesus' ministry, he proclaimed regeneration through repentance and faith available to all men. Later he established his church with a universal mission. When his missionary enterprise had been established and just before he returned to the Father, he called his followers to himself and commissioned them to give the message of his redemptive purpose to the entire world.

After the coming of the Holy Spirit on the day of Pentecost, the early Christians witnessed with great power and fervor. The New Testament churches were missionary because their members were missionary.

Paul and his missionary journeys are a part of the study of missions in the New Testament. In the first century, Paul became the great exponent of the missionary message of God's love to lost men in all countries. On these journeys he came face to face with the need of sinful men for regeneration.

Through a study of general and specific biblical teachings, members of WMU are made aware that the Bible is God's missionary message to mankind. The message is one of hope for sinful man. It is a message of missionary responsibility to a New Testament church. Woman's Missionary Union teaches this message to its members.

The Sunday School is a church's organization for teaching the biblical revelation. In this study, missions will emerge naturally as one of the dominant themes. From this base of Bible knowledge, Woman's Missionary Union leads persons into a specialized study of the missionary message of the Bible. This study majors on the missions theme, exploring the depths of its meaning and interpreting the full implications of its message.

(2) *Progress of Christian missions.*—A study of the missionary message of the Bible gives the basis for the world missions task of Baptists. A study of the progress of Christian missions is a study of the advance which has been made in carrying out the Great Commission of Christ. It is necessary for church members to know the conditions and circumstances under which the gospel has progressed from the ascension of Christ to the present. This can be achieved both through a general approach and a study of the history of missions in various countries.

The content area of Woman's Missionary Union includes the beginnings of missionary history in New Testament times. It encompasses the development of missionary history to the present. The study explores in depth the history of Baptist missions. This history includes an intensive study of missions from the time of William Carey to the present. An important section of this study is the development and progress of foreign missions under the leadership of the Foreign Mission Board of the Southern Baptist Convention.

The origin, development, and progress of Southern Baptist home missions under the direction of the Home Mission Board of the Southern Baptist Convention is another vital part of this study. The study of state and associational missions helps members comprehend the full missions task and missionary expression of the churches.

Because the content relating to the progress of Christian missions is so extensive, the approach of Woman's Missionary Union is the study of the most pivotal events and emphases in missionary history. Certain content is studied in regular lesson courses. Other phases of study find expression in mission study books.

Christian history is one of the content areas of the Training Union. The progress of Christian missions is a part of Christian history. While Training Union gives the broad historical base of Christianity, Woman's Missionary Union specializes in the missions aspect of this history. The approach lays the foundation for understanding the strategy and methods for contemporary missions. The comprehensive study of church history by the Training Union and the specialized study of the progress of Christian missions by Woman's Missionary Union and Brotherhood give church members proper balance, comprehensiveness, and sequence in study in these important content areas.

(3) *Contemporary missions.*—Although study of the biblical and historical material is necessary, a thorough study of the current situation must have full consideration by church members. The situation of missions today and in the future in one's association, state, nation, and in countries overseas must

be understood in order for church members to assess properly their role in missions.

The study of contemporary missions includes the philosophy of Christian missions, Southern Baptist missionary work, and the missionary work of other Christian groups. Missionary work can be understood only if the context in which it is undertaken is understood.

The content area of WMU deals with the philosophy of Christian missions. This study centers in the redemptive plan of God and the role of the Christian as an instrument of redemption. This study includes a rational defense of Christianity for persons who are under the influence of different cultures, religions, value systems, or philosophies of life. The study further deals with the various methods and techniques of Christian missions. There are many schools of thought regarding the best way to advance the cause of Christ. Some Christian groups expend all their resources in direct evangelism. Others have developed extensive medical and educational programs. This area of study helps Southern Baptists be aware of possible ways to communicate the gospel of Christ to the people of the world.

The study of other religions is a vital part of the study of missions. In addition to Christianity, there are ten living religions in the world today. Each of these religions has its own distinctive cultural setting and historical development. These factors as well as basic doctrinal beliefs determine the approach of Southern Baptist mission work among the people who adhere to the different religions.

The current work of the Home and Foreign Mission boards is the heart of the WMU content area. The work of the Foreign Mission Board is conducted in areas beyond the United States. The Home Mission Board, in cooperation with state conventions, assists Southern Baptist churches in their mission work at home. The varied missions approaches of these boards demonstrate versatility in meeting human need and in bringing men to God through Christ.

Southern Baptist missions work in the state and the association is part of the content area of missions. The materials to be used in this study are furnished by the state WMU or the state convention. A further area of Southern Baptist mission work is missions in the church community. WMU members study the principles and philosophy of missions in the immediate community which the church serves. These principles and this philosophy give direction for missions actions performed by WMU.

The study of the types, philosophy, and strategy of Southern Baptist missions work is incomplete without knowledge of the resources which make the work possible. These resources are prayer, personnel, and finances. Biblical and historical sources emphasize the place of prayer in the work of missions. The study concerning missionary personnel deals with biblical and historical sources setting forth the missionary implications of the Christian calling. This study further teaches the philosophy and procedure used by mission boards in sending out and supporting vocational missionaries. The material for the study of the financial support of missions includes the principles of stewardship of possessions and the media for supporting missions. These media are the church budget, the Cooperative Program, and the Lottie Moon and Annie Armstrong offerings.

A study of Southern Baptist resources takes into account the opportunities for training for missionary responsibility. WMU studies emphasize the place and importance of homes, churches, colleges, universities, and theological seminaries in missionary education.

WMU studies may include a look at the missions work of other Christian groups, such as other Baptist groups, other evangelicals and Protestants, Roman Catholics, and Orthodox Catholics. Obviously, a comprehensive study of these groups is impossible. WMU seeks to acquaint its members with the strategy and techniques employed by major Christian groups to propagate the gospel so that members can better understand forces at work in the world which affect Southern Baptist mission work.

The content area of WMU informs members of world conditions and trends affecting missions. These conditions and trends include economic, technological, spiritual, and sociocultural forces which affect the environment in which missions work is undertaken. On the national level, these same forces are at work. No two sections of this country are alike. They differ in political alignments; in economic, social, and educational levels; and in religious orientation. These and other environmental factors are studied in WMU as background for understanding Southern Baptist missionary work.

The content area of WMU brings together into a meaningful whole the missions content which emerges in other study programs, and gives major attention to contemporary missions. Only the mission organizations in the church deal regularly with contemporary missions in their study. WMU and Brotherhood uniquely serve the church in this important phase of the study of missions. Such resource materials as mission study books, missionary lesson courses, general missions books, misions magazines, and missionary biographies present this phase of the content area of these organizations.

2. *The Importance of Teaching Missions*

The study of missions is one of the most challenging of all study opportunities in a church. Each church should plan for missionary education to be offered to as many members as possible. The programs of Woman's Missionary Union and Brotherhood potentially offer missionary education to all church members.

The content area of Woman's Missionary Union can help a church achieve its reason for being. The study is designed to develop understanding of God's redemptive plan for all mankind. This understanding creates for a church an awareness of its mission in the world. The study of missions helps a church to recognize the universality of its mission and the scope of its responsibility.

The study of missions informs church members of their responsibility in the contemporary world. While the message of redemption is unchanging, the context in which the message is told is constantly changing. Church members must understand both the message and the contemporary world if they are to comprehend and accept their missionary task.

For church members the study of missions cultivates concern in the home, the community, and the world. Church members who are aware of the needs of the world for the gospel will overlook neither the needs nearest their door nor those farthest from their door. In most instances the church members who are shortsighted and ingrown in their concern are the church members who are not informed about the needs of lost persons around the world.

Missionary education stimulates the investment of lives and resources in missions. Knowledge of the need for missionaries will challenge young people to consider investing their lives in vocational missions service. The same information will challenge all church members to accept the missionary implications of their Christian calling, whatever their daily work may be. Appeals for financial and prayer support for missions are more effective when people understand their relationship to the world missions task. Many churches have not given their members the basic understandings of the stewardship of life out of which proper offerings come. Many Southern Baptist church members are still confined in thought and action to their own neighborhoods. They are often more concerned with themselves and their neighbors than with the needs of the multitudes of lost persons around the world. If these observations are true, it is because there has not been enough education and information to challenge them. The study of missions causes church members to lift up their eyes and look upon the fields and to respond to the needs they see.

II. Lead Persons to Participate in Missions

In addition to teaching missions, Woman's Missionary Union serves a church in other significant ways. WMU and Brotherhood lead church members to participate in missions. These two organizations have a responsibility to reach beyond their membership and involve all church members in missions actions. This means creating a learning environment which will help motivate missions concern and action. It further means planning ways church members can participate in missions actions.

1. *Relationships of Study and Other Actions in Woman's Missionary Union*

Studying about missions should lead to missions actions. Church members who are informed about missions needs are challenged to relate their lives and their resources to missions.

The involvement of church members in missions may be both spontaneous and planned. While a church member has many opportunities for spontaneous missions actions in response to the needs of persons, he must also see his responsibilities which can best be met as he relates to others in planned group activities. Woman's Missionary Union can lead church members into the spontaneous and the planned expressions of missions concern.

2. *Areas of Participation in Missions*

Woman's Missionary Union leads church members to participate in missions through praying, giving, witnessing, and ministering.

(1) *Praying for missions.*—Through intercessory prayer church members can labor alongside missionaries wherever they serve. They can be a part of all that Southern Baptists do to share the gospel.

An awareness of the physical, intellectual, social, and spiritual needs of individuals around the world should cause any thinking Christian to remember these multitudes of persons in prayer. When world needs are great and the money which is received for these needs is meager, one is led to pray that God may use these inadequate gifts as Jesus did the loaves and fishes. Certainly without the blessings of God, paltry gifts would never make much impact upon the tremendous needs of the world. One should pray also that new insights into the needs of persons without the gospel will cause Christians to share more of their material resources with these persons.

Prayer is perhaps the most neglected phase of a Christian's life. Most church members do not spend sufficient time in prayer. When they do pray, their prayers are so general that they hardly help those who have specific problems needing prayer support. There is value in concerted prayer and in praying for definite objects of need.

The Sunday School has the task of leading church members to worship daily. To the guidance in worship furnished by the Sunday School, Woman's Missionary Union adds the dimension of intercessory prayer for missions. WMU provides guides for individual, family, and corporate prayer for missions.

Woman's Missionary Union encourages church members to pray daily for missions, both individually and in family worship. Missionaries are listed on the prayer calendars in WMU magazines according to their birth dates. Their names, work, and fields of service are listed so that prayer for missions can be as specific as possible. As church members pray for missionaries daily, they can pray that the insights and the experiences of all Southern Baptists may lead them to develop an increasingly effective strategy for meeting the changing needs of today's world.

This organization engages church members in periods of special prayer during the annual weeks of prayer for home and foreign missions and the season of prayer for state missions.

Because Woman's Missionary Union has led persons to recognize the indispensable place of intercessory prayer, it is qualified to lead all church members into this significant spiritual experience.

(2) *Giving to missions.*—One of the most important ways Woman's Missionary Union serves a church is in leading members to be stewards of their possessions. Giving for the support of missions is both a privilege and a duty. Giving is a medium for the projection of oneself into the undertaking of world missions. The gift of money can be a gift of oneself. Gifts become the means of supporting missionaries, of building churches, of ministering to persons in hunger, sickness, ignorance, or other misfortune. Giving is meant to be an expression of obedience, faith, and sacrificial devotion.

Southern Baptists recognize that giving for the support of missions is but a part of the Christian's duty and privilege to support the varied aspects of the cause of Christ through the church. Woman's Missionary Union seeks to lead its members to this concept of unified giving. At the same time, this organization reminds the church of the primacy of world missions in its total stewardship responsibility.

Knowledge of missionaries' work and needs makes it possible for members of Woman's Missionary Union to give more intelligently to all causes through their church budget. To study missions and to pray for missions result in the desire to give to missions. Study and prayer personalize giving. Through study, Woman's Missionary Union members are made aware of the needs and problems of missions work and learn the names and vocations of the missionaries. Giving money through the church budget is then visualized as a means of assisting a missionary doctor or nurse in Japan, a theological professor in Taiwan, or a missionary pastor in Argentina.

In addition to this support through the church budget, Woman's Missionary Union leads its members and other church members to give beyond the tithe through the Convention-approved special mission offerings. These are the Annie Armstrong Offering, the Lottie Moon Christmas Offering, and the state missions offering.

Members of this organization also study carefully the Cooperative Program and the causes it includes. Program materials of Woman's Missionary Union carry information regarding the Southern Baptist Convention agencies which are supported through the Cooperative Program. Knowledge of their work and needs leads to increased support of the Cooperative Program.

While all organizations of the church have a responsibility in stewardship, Woman's Missionary Union keeps before the church its potential and its responsibility for setting forward the purpose of God around the world.

3. *Missions Actions*

Woman's Missionary Union is aware that when missions concern is genuine, it will find expression in the immediate community. Praying and giving are essential, but members must also become personally involved in ministering and in witnessing to persons in their communities.

In every community there are groups of people who will never be reached for the church without special ministries. Because of certain economic, physical, cultural, and social barriers these persons often require a specialized ministry beyond the church's direct outreach efforts. The church is responsible for these people. They include migrants, illiterates, deaf, blind, international students, refugees, language and racial groups, juvenile delinquents, the imprisoned, institutionalized, and others. Members of Woman's Missionary Union can serve Christ and his church by ministering to the needs of these persons and by witnessing to them of his love. Meeting these needs will require a variety of activities. These activities include such things as conducting mission Sunday Schools, mission Bible classes, and mission Vacation Bible Schools; engaging in personal ministries based on individual needs; and establishing or assisting with mission-center type work. Some of these persons will eventually become members of churches; others will continue to require the churches' ministry of a self-giving nature.

Another type of missions action of Woman's Missionary Union deals with strengthening Christian standards in each community. Distributing Bibles and Christian literature, supporting alcohol education, engaging in activities related to responsible citizenship, and strengthening moral standards are a part of missions actions.

A task of Sunday School is to lead in reaching all prospects for the church. Missions actions conducted by Woman's Missionary Union and Brotherhood must be understood in proper relationship to this task. The Sunday School structures the church's direct outreach efforts that are beamed toward sustaining the church. Woman's Missionary Union and Brotherhood participate in this effort. At the same time these two organizations minister and witness to persons of special need or circumstances who are not immediate prospects for the church. In this way a church both sustains its own life and moves out to share its life-giving source with others.

Another task of the Sunday School is to lead church members to worship, witness, learn, and minister daily. WMU encourages members to take advantage of spontaneous witnessing opportunities in the home and community. But personal involvement in missionary effort means that members of Woman's Missionary Union take part in the church program of witnessing. They do this by participating in the ongoing personal witnessing engaged in by the church and structured primarily by the Sunday School. In contrast, the Sunday School ministers primarily to the church membership and majors on the spontaneous approach. WMU majors on the planned approach to ministry to persons of special need in the community.

III. PROVIDE ORGANIZATION AND LEADERSHIP FOR SPECIAL MISSIONS PROJECTS OF THE CHURCH

Woman's Missionary Union serves the church by conducting special projects. These projects usually involve churchwide participation in missionary activity.

1. *The Nature and Purpose of Special Projects*

The two tasks of Woman's Missionary Union already discussed suggest study and action on a continuing basis to help the church fulfil its missions responsibilities. These tasks involve members in a steady, continuous experience vital to Christian growth and service. In contrast, the third task of WMU is an assignment of responsibility of projects of short-term duration. Missions projects are special jobs the church wants to do at a given time. Woman's Missionary Union stands ready to use its resources to conduct missions projects for the church.

The missions projects which a church asks Woman's Missionary Union to conduct should grow out of the other tasks of the organization. They will relate to missions. This principle can help a church distribute its work load in the best possible way. For example, the church may need a churchwide missions study. It is logical that it would turn to Woman's Missionary Union and Brotherhood to provide organization and leadership for this project. Since one of the major tasks of these organizations is teaching missions, they should be best equipped to lead the church in missions study.

Missions projects support the ongoing program of Woman's Missionary Union. Although the organization may need at a given time to concentrate most of its resources on a missions project, the ongoing work of the organization is not interrupted. This concentration of resources will be temporary. Ultimately the project serves to give new thrust and incentive to the ongoing work of the church. An example of this principle is the observance of the weeks of prayer. Woman's Missionary Union concentrates its resources to make these weeks vital spiritual experiences for the church and a help to world missions. When the projects are completed, their benefits linger. The church feels a new incentive to pray for missions, renewed eagerness to learn about missions needs, and greater faithfulness in giving. Woman's Missionary Union members will be more faithful to daily intercessory prayer.

2. *Special Missions Projects Led by Woman's Missionary Union*

Woman's Missionary Union has traditionally provided organization and leadership for two types of projects: the weeks of prayer and special missions offerings.

During the Week of Prayer for Foreign Missions and the Week of Prayer for Home Missions, church members are encouraged to concentrate on the missions work God is guiding Southern Baptists to do. They pray with renewed devotion and give to the Lottie Moon Christmas Offering and the Annie Armstrong Offering. Each church which participates in these projects finds its interest in, and its support of, world missions increasing. By remembering the definite objects of prayer for foreign and home missions, thousands of church members mobilize their prayer potential. By making the offerings churchwide, WMU strengthens church and denominational life. These special weeks of study, prayer, and giving are significant times for missions each year. Woman's Missionary

Union has requested and receives support from the other church program organizations in the promotion of these projects.

Missions projects which the church will assign to WMU are not limited to these two well-known projects. Other possibilities include the teaching of missions books and service projects for persons in need in the community, state, nation, and in countries overseas. Any missions project relating to teaching missions, praying for missions, giving to support missions, and ministering and witnessing to persons of special need could logically be carried out by Woman's Missionary Union.

Woman's Missionary Union and Brotherhood take the lead in conducting missions projects for the church. These organizations support and participate in all other projects undertaken by the church or any of its organizations. For example, WMU participates in special revival efforts and other evangelistic activities of the church.

Each church program organization is responsible for projects. In conducting all projects, the centrality of the church is the focal point. But the significance of each organization is quickly apparent. Each organization stands ready to use its organization and leadership to do the jobs the church considers most urgent at a given time. Each program maintains its distinctiveness as it provides organization and leadership for projects that grow out of its tasks. At the same time, it helps the church do its total work in an efficient manner.

IV. PROVIDE AND INTERPRET INFORMATION REGARDING THE WORK OF THE CHURCH AND THE DENOMINATION

Woman's Missionary Union serves the church as an agent of communication. All church members need to be informed of various projects and emphases as well as programs to which they should be vitally related. Officers in Woman's Missionary Union, by keeping in close contact with the pastor and other workers of the church, assist in informing the members of their organization about church plans and programs. WMU magnifies the total program of the church and gives first consideration to its life and work. By interpreting information for the church, each Woman's Missionary Union fulfils its task in an effective way.

As a member of the church council, the president of Woman's Missionary Union knows the total church program and assists not only in planning it but also in interpreting it to the leaders and members of WMU. Members should be led to see that each church organization must function properly if Christ's work is to be done in a significant way. Such special occasions as revivals, church budget subscriptions, church building campaigns, and special weeks of study should be presented in general meetings and members should be encouraged to give their full support to them. Any concern of the church should be the concern of each church organization.

Leaders of WMU unit organizations and circles should be given information regarding church activities so that it may be shared with all Woman's Missionary Union members in their meetings. Keeping members informed of their church's work can involve them in the basic actions which the church will take throughout the year.

Although it majors on teaching missions and leading persons to participate in missions, Woman's Missionary Union is valuable both to the churches and to the denomination in interpreting information regarding other programs. Through its periodicals, WMU interprets the programs of other Southern Baptist Convention agencies. In addition to the regular program materials, such information is studied by members of this organization. WMU assists Southern Baptist Convention agencies which do not have organization in the states and associations to carry their programs to the churches.

A case in point is the Stewardship Commission of the Southern Baptist Convention. This commission was established to coordinate and promote activities related to church finance and the Cooperative Program. The Stewardship Commission has no corresponding church organization through which to work. Woman's Missionary Union can both interpret the work of this commission and assist other church program organizations, such as the Sunday School and Training Union, in providing an educational and informational base for the Stewardship Commission's program activities.

A major role of Woman's Missionary Union is to communicate the programs of the Home Mission Board and the Foreign Mission Board to church members. In addition to curriculum materials which interpret the actual missions work engaged in by these boards, Woman's Missionary Union materials interpret the manner in which these boards are organized and function. Woman's Missionary Union members are informed of the plan of operation of these agencies, the financial requirements for program operations, the unmet needs which they face, and the resources available to the church from each board. This information not only personalizes those who serve in these agencies but also causes Woman's Missionary Union members to become identified with the missionaries who serve under the appointment of these boards.

Each program organization in the church is responsible for serving the church as a channel of communication. To the degree that each of these organizations does this, church members will be informed and alert to the opportunities and challenges of their church and their denomination.

The continuing program of Woman's Missionary Union in the church is to teach missions and to engage church members in participation in missions at home and abroad. In helping the church fulfil the mission for which Christ established it, Woman's Missionary Union works closely with all other church organizations, and with the pastor and church staff. Within the fellowship of the church, Woman's Missionary Union members experience the full meaning of their watchword, "Labourers together with God" (1 Cor. 3:9).

Every Baptist church will find that its task of becoming a missionary church will be accomplished much more readily and effectively if it supports and uses its Woman's Missionary Union.

CHAPTER 7

I. TEACH MISSIONS TO ALL MEN, YOUNG MEN, AND BOYS

1. Teach the Missionary Message of the Bible
2. Teach the Role of the Church in Missions
3. Teach the History of Christian Missions
4. Teach Contemporary Missions

II. LEAD ALL MEN, YOUNG MEN, AND BOYS TO PARTICIPATE IN MISSIONS ACTIVITIES

1. Pray for Missions
2. Give to Missions
3. Participate in Missions Actions

III. PROVIDE ORGANIZATION AND LEADERSHIP FOR SPECIAL PROJECTS OF THE CHURCH

1. Provide Organization and Leadership in Revival Activities
2. Provide Organization and Leadership in Special Missions Offerings
3. Lead Men in Stewardship Actions
4. Help Strengthen Churches
5. Provide Leadership for Missions Projects Outside the Community

IV. PROVIDE AND INTERPRET INFORMATION REGARDING THE WORK OF THE CHURCH AND THE DENOMINATION

1. Interpret the Work of the Church
2. Interpret the Work of the Convention Agencies
3. Interpret Annual Denominational Emphases

7

The Brotherhood Program
of a Church

BROTHERHOOD is the church's educational organization which provides missionary education for men, young men, and boys. Units of Brotherhood organization are Baptist Men, responsible for missionary education for men twenty-five years and older; Baptist Young Men for young men between the ages eighteen and twenty-four; and Royal Ambassadors for boys nine through seventeen years of age.

The Southern Baptist Convention established the close relationship between Brotherhood and missionary education in June, 1965, when it approved the following objective for Brotherhood work:

"The objective of the Brotherhood Commission is to support the Southern Baptist Convention in its task of bringing men to God through Christ by fostering programs that will assist the churches in their tasks of leading men, young men, and boys to a deeper commitment to missions, to a more meaningful prayer life for missions, to a larger stewardship on behalf of missions, and to a personal involvement in missions."

To implement this mandate, the Brotherhood Commission is providing materials and other aids to help churches fulfil their responsibility in missionary education and missions involvement through Brotherhood.

The work of a church is not many separate, independent programs but one program made up of smaller related programs assigned by the church to organizations. As a part of the church's total program, the Brotherhood functions in relationship to the other organizations of a church.

To provide unity, all the work of a Brotherhood should be correlated with the other church educational organizations—Sunday School, Training Union, Woman's Missionary Union, and Music Ministry—and appropriate church committees. The best way for achieving this correlation is through a church council.

The very nature of a New Testament church supports the need to enlist all men, young men, and boys in missionary education and missions activities.

The New Testament teaches that a church is a body of baptized believers, in covenant with God and one another, for the presenting of the gospel of Jesus Christ to all people of the world with the purpose of leading them to personal faith in Christ and obedience to his will. Such a definition embodies the mission of a church.

Missions may be defined as what the church is and does to achieve its mission in all areas of human need which are on the growing edge of the church's confrontation with the non-Christian world.

For men, young men, and boys, missions is extending the gospel beyond the congregation. While the Sunday School is reaching prospects for the church, the Brotherhood will be reaching people who have continuing mission needs. To accomplish this purpose, the church Brotherhood provides missionary education for men, young men, and boys.

Missionary education is that part of Christian education which majors on interpreting the missionary message of the Bible and the course of Christian missions.

Involvement in missionary education is an understanding of physical and spiritual needs at home and around the world and a readiness to meet these needs. Basic also is an enlarging knowledge of other races and groups and a willingness to share with them the Christian message.

Missionary education describes a man's relationship to God and an understanding of Christ's love and purpose for all men.

The scope of missionary education for Brotherhood includes God's missionary purpose for mankind as expressed in the Bible, a knowledge of how the Christian message is being shared with the world, and an explanation of how it must be shared with every generation.

The study of the spread of the gospel is designed to challenge men, young men, and boys to participate in the extension of Christ's kingdom on earth.

The Brotherhood program also places a continuing emphasis on the need to develop and channel the concern of Baptist men, young men, and boys to an application of their faith through service in their church, community, and world.

Like other programs carried out by organizations, the Brotherhood program is composed of church tasks. They are (1) teach missions to all men, young men, and boys; (2) lead all men, young men, and boys to participate in mission activities; (3) provide organization and leadership for special projects of the church; and (4) interpret the work of the church and the denomination.

I. TEACH MISSIONS TO ALL MEN, YOUNG MEN, AND BOYS

Teaching the missionary message of the Bible is the task of a church. Jesus commanded his church: "Teaching them to observe all things whatsoever I have commanded you" (Matt. 28:20). The Brotherhood program is designed to help the church fulfil its missionary education responsibilities. To do this, the Brotherhood centers its study on the biblical basis for world missions.

The study emphasizes strongly the role of the church in the missionary movement and activities in all areas of the world as well as all people of the earth. Also essential in understanding the mission of the church is knowing the history of Christian missions, how Southern Baptist mission boards function, and how Southern Baptists finance missions work.

1. *Teach the Missionary Message of the Bible*

The Bible is a missionary book with a missionary message that runs from Genesis through Revelation.

God's universal purpose from the beginning of history has been to love and redeem all mankind. The Old and New

Testaments reveal God and his plan for using man to accomplish his purpose.

The Bible is an account of God's concern for man's redemption. It records the establishment of the church with a universal mission and the commissioning of every Christian to take part in this task.

In teaching missions, the Brotherhood seeks to lead its members to an understanding of the scriptural imperative of world missions (Matt. 28: 19–20; Acts 1: 8).

2. *Teach the Role of the Church in Missions*

The church is at the heart of all missions work. Repeatedly Paul said the church is "the body of Christ" (Rom. 12:5; 1 Cor. 12:27; Eph. 1:23). As the body of Christ, the church is seeking to continue Christ's mission on earth. To be a member of today's New Testament church should mean that a member is directly involved in what Christ is doing in the world. In a study of missions, men and boys will have opportunities to see the greatness of the New Testament church as it is revealed in the Scriptures and their responsibilities as church members in contemporary life.

A further study of Christians and their relationship to world redemption reveals that salvation is a call to service. Jesus said, "Ye have not chosen me, but I have chosen you, and ordained you, that ye should go and bring forth fruit" (John 15:16).

Christians are saved to become the trophies of God's redemption in Christ. They are also saved to become the instruments of God's redemption.

Faith must be productive. That characteristic is inherent in the nature of Christian faith. Faith is also creative in the sense that moral and spiritual results spring from it. "Faith without works is dead" (James 2:20).

Christians are judged by their deeds. It was Paul who said that everyone should give an account of himself to God (Rom. 14:12). He also said all must appear before God in a judgment that each one may receive what is due him. Such words should compel Christians to spend their lives in service and devotion to Jesus Christ.

The Christian reaches his highest point of dedication when he learns to deny himself for others. This kind of discipleship should be a characteristic of every Christian.

To be a member of Christ's body is to be involved in what Christ is doing on the earth. "And whether one member suffer, all the members suffer with it; or one member be honoured, all the members rejoice with it" (1 Cor. 12:26). This same relationship would be true in service and involvement.

The nature of the body as an organism implies work and service. "And the eye cannot say unto the hand, I have no need of thee" (1 Cor. 12:21). Each is expected to serve in his capacity. Each should be enlisted and involved to serve in his own capacity. The body cannot function properly without the eyes, the hands, and the feet. A church cannot function properly without the full enlistment of its men in missions. The church that neglects its men is not performing within the will of Christ.

3. *Teach the History of Christian Missions*

The missions cause became a world movement with the command of Jesus Christ (Matt. 28:19–20). Its first one hundred years of progress is recorded in the New Testament.

Missionary education for men, young men, and boys includes a study of the development of Christian missions through the centuries.

The history of Baptist missions, including the origin and development of foreign, home, state, and associational missions, receives particular attention.

A study of the hardships early Baptists faced in establishing an aggressive missions program should build among men, young men, and boys an appreciation for Baptists' heritage and point up the need for more male members of the church to take part in missions.

4. *Teach Contemporary Missions*

The church Brotherhood helps its constituency see vividly the expanding missions programs of Southern Baptists.

A depth study of missions today can build an awareness

of mission needs for tomorrow and motivate Christian men and boys to see that these needs are met.

(1) *Teach how missions work is done.*—Southern Baptist missions work centers in each church. Yet one church alone cannot meet all mission needs around the world. Churches unite to form associations, state conventions, and the Southern Baptist Convention in order to carry out the Great Commission. Their joint efforts comprise Southern Baptist missions work.

The church Brotherhood has the responsibility of interpreting to men, young men, and boys the objectives and programs of the associations, state conventions, and the mission boards of the Southern Baptist Convention.

(2) *Interpret the program for financing Southern Baptist missions work.*—Since 1925, Southern Baptist churches have supported missions through the Cooperative Program. This plan arose out of the efforts of churches to find a plan whereby all worthy denominational causes might be cared for fairly.

The Cooperative Program presents to Southern Baptists a sane, scriptural, comprehensive, unifying, equitable, economical, and thoroughly workable plan for advancing God's work.

II. Lead All Men, Young Men, and Boys to Participate in Missions Activities

God speaks to individuals and leads them into missions activities. Out of Bible study there comes an understanding of God's nature, concern, and love for a lost world. The fulness of God's compassion is revealed in Jesus Christ. An intimate knowledge of Jesus and his sacrificial love stirs the converted heart. Out of this depth of knowledge comes motivation to give oneself in missions actions.

1. *Pray for Missions*

Prayer deepens the concern of men, young men, and boys for missions. Intercessory prayer for work of the church, missions, missionaries, and the mission boards is a vital missions activity for Baptist men and boys. The Southern Baptist world missions program is undergirded through prayer periods at Brotherhood organizational meetings and special prayer fellowships.

Prayer should support every mission activity. All Brotherhood units not only pray for associational, state, home, and foreign missions, but through prayer they prepare to launch and sustain church missions projects, missions seminars, and pioneer mission crusades.

Prayer is an important activity in every Brotherhood program because of what it can do for those who pray as well as for those for whom they are praying.

2. *Give to Missions*

The church Brotherhood seeks to involve every man and boy by leading them to support missions with their tithes and offerings.

Men and boys become aware of the need of missions work in their community and around the world through the study of missions and by taking part in missions activities. Because of this awakened interest and understanding, there is personal concern for missions work and a desire to become more vitally related to it.

3. *Participate in Missions Actions*

(1) *Witness in missions situations.*—The heart of Jesus' ministry on earth was his personal witness to the unsaved. Jesus witnessed on the highway, beside a well, in a home, on the slope of a mountain, and to a thief on a cross. Witnessing is evidence of new life and faith in a Christian.

Today's world is one of travel and change. Thousands of men leave home on Monday and don't return until Saturday. They go because their job or business demands it. Overseas travel for business and pleasure continues to increase.

Baptist men can find some unusual opportunities to witness as they travel. In a sense, the man riding a plane can become a mission field to a Baptist man sitting beside him. This is also true of the taxi driver, the hotel doorman, the new business acquaintance, or the person in the next bus seat. In this relationship, each man is a missionary.

More and more men and boys are thinking of their daily witness and are coming to understand that the call to Christ is a call to witness on the job, in the home, and through other facets of life. People without Christ, regardless of their relationship to the believer, have the primary need of redemption through Christ.

(2) *Lead in family life education and witnessing.*—As husband and father, a man is responsible for the spiritual growth of his family. Baptist Men should present family-related programs and actions to help men build strong Christian homes.

Men have a responsibility to teach their families the importance of the stewardship of life, including giving as it relates to family budgets. Family budgets should be arranged in accordance with priority needs.

A man should lead his family in making the home an outpost of evangelism. Families may begin by witnessing to other families in the community. Homes also should be used to reach special groups such as international students and Jewish families.

From time to time the Brotherhood Commission will develop special materials emphasizing the importance of the family in witnessing to families and individuals. These materials also will be produced in consultation with the Family Life Department of the Sunday School Board and the Division of Evangelism of the Home Mission Board.

(3) *Lead worship activities in missions areas.*—The hunger and thirst of people for God often can only be met through worship. There is a need for men to lead worship services in institutions and other areas of the community.

When people will not attend the worship services in the church building, the church must go to the people. The Brotherhood organizations can help provide these mission opportunities. A church Baptist Men's organization can help organize and lead worship services, prayer meetings, and testimonial fellowship in jails, rest homes, police and fire stations, homes, and even rented buildings in mission areas.

(4) *Organize and lead educational activities in mission areas.*—There are many opportunities for missions actions that

include Bible teaching and training. Men can help organize work with illiterates. Teaching people to read can be a means of teaching the Bible. The influx of language groups into urban communities offers an opportunity to teach English, and at the same time, teach the Bible.

Organizing mission Bible classes in homes, trailer parks, factories, and high-rise apartments are challenges to men.

There also is a need in Mission Centers for men to teach the Bible, thereby helping meet the needs of other people.

Royal Ambassadors may plan chapter meetings in missions areas and invite boys to attend as their guests.

Some actions may result in establishing a mission Sunday School or a Bible class. When this need arises, the work should be carried out in relationship to the Sunday School program.

(5) *Minister to persons with special needs.*—Churches should serve the needs of people in their communities. Many of these community needs can be met through the Brotherhood organizations. They may include social problems arising from juvenile rehabilitation, deserted children, alcoholism, migrant workers, breadwinners in prison, and non-English-speaking groups.

Men are expected to try to help solve the community problems of unemployment, poverty, school dropouts, and illiteracy. Boys through individual and chapter service projects also can help the needy in their neighborhood and community.

Many churches have neglected those people victimized by earthquakes, fire, and floods. Brotherhood members can help these people in the name of Christ.

(6) *Help start missions.*—To help fulfil the task of leading all men, young men, and boys in mission activities, Baptist Men may start new Sunday Schools, Extension Bible classes, and mission Vacation Bible Schools in mission areas on assignment from the church. This work is coordinated through the church council with that of other organizations and committees. The Brotherhood and WMU will work closely with the church missions committee and the church Sunday School in performing this work.

The church's local missions program offers many opportunities to use the resources of men. For instance, Baptist Men can help take mission surveys at the request of the missions committee. Men can donate materials and labor for new church buildings, chapels, and meeting places for church extension.

(7) *Help meet citizenship needs.*—Many Baptist men are interested in strengthening moral standards in their community, state, and nation through their Christian influence.

With the help of the pastor, Baptist Men can deal with community evils, including violations of the principles of separation of church and state, alcohol problems, juvenile problems, lack of law enforcement, and actions by local government which adversely affect the community.

Baptist Men encourage members to exercise Christian citizenship by taking a more active role in civic organization, public office, and other practical places of service in community life where men may lend Christian influence.

III. Provide Organization and Leadership for Special Projects of the Church

As an organization serves the church, there will be church projects that demand the enlistment of men, young men, and boys. The church will find planning easier when it uses men and boys in existing organizations. Churches which coordinate their work through the church council should have no difficulty with planning and promotion.

Projects have a definite beginning and ending time. They are not considered as the ongoing week-after-week or month-after-month work of a church.

1. *Provide Organization and Leadership in Revival Activities*

The church revival is a project that demands the total effort of all church organizations. There are many types of church revivals. However, most churches have annual or semiannual revivals with an emphasis on winning lost people. All revival plans should be worked out in coordination with church organizations.

Unless the evangelistic services are laymen sponsored, the Brotherhood will do its best work in a supportive role. Men can be enlisted to lead neighborhood prayer meetings and participate in all-night prayer services. Men and boys can be used to park automobiles and distribute revival announcements and posters. Men also can provide transportation to the revival for shut-ins and people with special needs, such as the handicapped or elderly.

2. *Provide Organization and Leadership in Special Missions Offerings*

Church Brotherhood units should participate fully in special missions offerings. These offerings do not replace the weekly offerings of men and boys. They should be promoted as opportunities for sacrificial giving.

In many churches, there will be joint promotion by Woman's Missionary Union and Brotherhood. This also could include joint mission study and joint seasons of prayer.

Special missions offerings present an effective approach for helping develop mission-minded men and boys.

Brotherhood programs personalize missions. Knowledge of mission fields and missionaries and a special emphasis on the seasons of prayer, including giving to the Lottie Moon Christmas Offering for foreign missions and the Annie Armstrong Offering for home missions, are important parts of Brotherhood work.

Churches participating in state missions offerings should offer Brotherhood members the opportunity of participation.

3. *Lead Men in Stewardship Actions*

It is impossible to teach missions without teaching that missions requires a person's all—his life. This is Christian stewardship. The Brotherhood plays a supportive role in stewardship by participating in the church's stewardship goals. Like evangelism, stewardship is a part of all that a church is seeking to accomplish.

There are supportive actions for men. These actions include participation in the yearly stewardship emphasis and church budget campaigns. The Brotherhood units are ideal groups to provide manpower for tithing testimonies in worship services and organizational assemblies. As head of their homes, men have a way of impressing other Christians through tithing testimonies. Men should be enlisted to lead in a prayer emphasis prior to the adoption of a church budget and on budget subscription Sunday. The use of men in these stewardship activities is more fully explained in the materials of the Stewardship Commission of the Southern Baptist Convention or the state stewardship department.

4. *Help Strengthen Churches*

Our moving society has left many rural churches with a small number of active members. These congregations could be served by qualified men either in laymen's revivals or through planned visitation in the church community. Many retired men could give themselves to full-time service as they are led by the Holy Spirit to serve as pastors and visitors for these churches. However, men entering this area of work should be certain God is leading them.

When requested, strong units of Baptist Men should offer the services of men to churches without recent baptisms. The Training Union could prepare these men to serve these churches with the appropriate training.

Baptist churches should work through associational leaders in carrying out this project.

5. *Provide Leadership for Missions Projects Outside the Community*

Southern Baptist churches through the Brotherhood Commission and state Brotherhood departments have periodic opportunities to send men and boys to mission fields for service and a firsthand report on missions progress. The missions seminars and service opportunities may be in another association or state, a pioneer section of the United States, or in foreign countries, yet they should be church related. Churches should take special interest in these missions projects.

Men and boys who have participated in missions seminars

and projects usually return home deeply motivated with a greater desire to serve Christ.

The work reports of the men and boys and their enthusiasm create a new spirit of missions in the churches.

With few exceptions, Baptist men, young men, and boys have made good impressions upon the citizens of the countries they have visited.

Baptist Men also can help the church carry out missions projects by encouraging men during their vacation trips each year to visit sites of state, home, and foreign mission work.

Many Baptist businessmen are making trips to foreign lands each year. Churches overlook a missions opportunity in not asking these men to visit Baptist mission areas on the trips and tell about them when they return.

The Brotherhood organizations encourage men to take advantage of missions opportunities in the armed forces. Many career men in the armed services are discovering valuable opportunities to witness for Christ.

In addition, men in churches near military installations find that working with the chaplains and military personnel in special projects is spiritually gratifying. However, the chaplains and military personnel should express a desire for this help before it is given.

Participation in projects within a state and in pioneer missions projects is another source of Christian expression for Baptist men. These projects call for laymen to go into areas of their state or the United States where Baptist work is weak to help the associational or area missionaries and church members strengthen the Baptist witness. Sometimes it means establishing new missions. At other times, it is taking a religious census or witnessing from door to door. Again it may mean working to provide facilities for a Baptist church or mission or engaging in laymen-sponsored revivals and crusades.

Many missions projects of the church need the specific help of young men. For instance, some churches use young men to conduct mission Vacation Bible Schools.

With a little encouragement from Baptist Young Men,

young college men will volunteer as student summer missionaries under the auspices of the Home Mission Board and Baptist Student Union.

A spirit of missions can be created within the congregation if a church will give its young men opportunities to tell of their summer experience.

Some churches are enlarging the scope of their ministry by encouraging young men to look for opportunities of Christian service while away from home and asking them to report on this service when they return. Many young men who leave their home churches and go into other parts of the United States find as many opportunities for mission work as those who travel to other countries.

At home, young men can serve Christ well as counselors in summer camps. Adept at speaking the language of boys, these young men can guide many youngsters to Christ and to future Christian service in an outdoor atmosphere.

IV. PROVIDE AND INTERPRET INFORMATION REGARDING THE WORK OF THE CHURCH AND THE DENOMINATION

The Brotherhood organizations interpret basic information regarding the work of the church and the denomination.

1. *Interpret the Work of the Church*

It is important for every member of a church to know the fulness of the church's ministry. The Brotherhood organizations will use the Brotherhood council to keep its constituency informed. The council is made up of leaders from each of the three units—Baptist Men, Baptist Young Men, and Royal Ambassadors. Through the Brotherhood council, all the work of these organizations will be coordinated in keeping with the total work of the church.

2. *Interpret the Work of Convention Agencies*

Other church program organizations have this same task. Each program organization will seek to interpret the work of the denomination through its curriculum materials.

The Brotherhood Commission cooperates with other Convention agencies in channeling information about the denomination to men, young men, and boys.

3. *Interpret Annual Denominational Emphases*

The Southern Baptist Convention develops a theme each year to emphasize a particular phase of church work. Each agency of the Convention seeks to relate to this annual emphasis with study material and actions.

Through Brotherhood, the Brotherhood Commission seeks to make the annual emphasis significant to men, young men, and boys in the area of missions.

CHAPTER 8

I. PROVIDE MUSIC AND MUSICIANS FOR THE CONGREGATIONAL SERVICES AND THE ORGANIZATIONS OF THE CHURCH
  1. Congregational Services of the Church
  2. Organizational Services of the Church

II. LEAD PERSONS TO PARTICIPATE IN HYMN SINGING
  1. Congregational Participation
  2. Organizational Participation
  3. Family Living
  4. Varied Occasions

III. TEACH MUSIC AND HYMNODY
  1. Graded Choirs
  2. Music and Hymnology Classes
  3. Instrumental

IV. TRAIN PERSONS TO LEAD, SING, AND PLAY MUSIC
  1. Training Persons to Lead Singing
  2. Training Persons to Sing
  3. Training Persons to Play Instruments

V. PROVIDE ORGANIZATION FOR LEADERSHIP FOR SPECIAL PROJECTS OF THE CHURCH

VI. PROVIDE AND INTERPRET INFORMATION REGARDING THE WORK OF THE CHURCH AND THE DENOMINATION

8

The Music Program
of a Church

MUSIC has always been identified with worship. From the earliest biblical times to the present the singing of God's people has been a dynamic part of their religion. Through the lifting of their voices in praise, adoration, thanksgiving, petition, and confession, the hearts of men have been drawn closer to their Creator.

Music characterizes Christianity. The coming of Christ was attended by the singing of the heavenly hosts. His going to the cross was preceded by the singing of a hymn with his disciples at the Last Supper. Christians have sung of their Saviour and their religion through the ages. Wherever Christianity is known today, it is known as the singing religion.

Music is meaningful in churches today. Through hymn singing, choral music, instrumental music, and the use of various musical forms, the people participate in church activities. With music being so traditionally a part of worship, proclamation, education, and ministry, all churches continue to use it today because of its proved effectiveness in involving people in these functions.

While all churches use music in some form in the various functions, not all churches make a conscious effort to assure a growing usefulness of music in their future. Concern for the effectiveness of worship and maximum participation on the part of the people in worship should stimulate desire for an increasingly effective use of music. Such a desire calls for some type of organized effort to involve people in music understanding and training.

The Southern Baptist Convention as early as 1925 recognized the need for a music education program as it grew concerned over the music in the churches that comprise the Convention. This concern took note of the expanding use of music in schools, radio, community concerts, civic bands and orchestras, recordings, and the growing music enlightenment of our society. After detailed study, the Convention acted in 1944 to establish a program of church music at the Sunday School Board which would assist the churches in establishing, conducting, enlarging, and improving their music programs. Such action provides helpful program resources for each church desiring to grow musically.

A church desiring a Bible teaching program usually organizes a Sunday School. Desire for a training program usually results in a Training Union. Missionary programs find expression in Woman's Missionary Union and in Brotherhood. Desire for a music program is usually expressed through organizing a Music Ministry. It is possible to have music in the church without having an organized Music Ministry, but to assure a growing effectiveness of music for the future an organized effort is desirable. In order to insure better hymn singing, train choir singers, develop instrumentalists, and increase understanding of hymns and an appreciation of music in all areas of church life, a Music Ministry should be organized. Responsibility for developing the music in the church needs to be firmly established.

A church establishes a Music Ministry when it elects a music director and charges him with the responsibility for developing a music program for the church. It also elects others to serve with him, usually a church pianist and/or organist, and others who will serve in various leadership capacities. The program will be designed to serve not only the worship services but also all areas of church life.

The music program of the church is given tasks to perform for the church. These tasks define its areas of operation and constitute the work of the Music Ministry. These tasks are:

1. Provide music and musicians for the congregational services and the organizations of the church

2. Lead persons to participate in hymn singing
3. Teach music and hymnody
4. Train persons to lead, sing, and play music
5. Provide organization and leadership for special projects of the church
6. Provide and interpret information regarding the work of the church and denomination

We shall examine carefully these tasks in order to have a clear understanding of them. As they are enumerated, relationship to the congregation as a whole, to organizations, and to various groups and services will be explained.

I. PROVIDE MUSIC AND MUSICIANS FOR THE CONGREGATIONAL SERVICES AND THE ORGANIZATIONS OF THE CHURCH

The Music Ministry ministers to every person in the church. It should work to improve music in all the congregational services and the church organizations. It should lead every member of the church and its organizations to participate actively in music and to understand the appropriateness, the meaning, and the significance of music in all church life. It should make possible increasing appreciation of the various music forms used and make good listeners as well as good participants of church members. It should help focus the attention of worshipers on the object of their worship and should lead each person into a deeper experience of worship.

1. *Congregational Services of the Church*

Congregational services are defined as any gathering together of the people—worship services, prayer meetings, revivals, special days, and miscellaneous meetings. In the congregational services there will be music experiences which include participation in congregational hymn singing and listening to instrumental and choral music performed by choirs, ensembles, and soloists. Multiple opportunities exist for the worship of God through music and for expressing one's praise, adoration, testimony, and thanksgiving through participation in music.

In most churches, music of some form constitutes 35 to 45 percent of the worship service time. Detailed plans for this music must be made by the pastor and the music director prior to each service so as to make possible orderly progression and more meaningful experience on the part of the worshipers. Themes to be developed, emphases to be given, and atmosphere to be desired do not often occur without prior design and prayerful planning. Each service should be characterized by music that is appropriate, worshipful, and meaningful for the gathering of God's people to worship in spirit and in truth.

Musicians provided for the congregational services include those who lead congregational singing, direct choirs, play instruments, sing in choral groups or ensembles or as soloists, and any other personnel who may have music responsibility. As each performs his responsibility, it should be evident to the worshipers that prayerful preparation, dedicated service, and a desire to make worship more meaningful for each person attending is an expression of the Music Ministry of the church.

In order to make possible this task the church must recognize that materials and equipment are necessary for the Music Ministry. These include such things as an adequate supply of hymnals, graded choir music, choir robes, instrumental music, physical facilities for the choirs, hymnal racks on the pews, and essential instruments such as organ and piano. Appropriate and adequate music supplies and equipment complement the provision of music and musicians for the congregational services. Their use and proper maintenance help sustain the proper level of participation and performance.

2. *Organizational Services of the Church*

The second half of the first task is to provide music and musicians for the organizations of the church. This has reference to all the program organizations and other organized activities in which music and musicians are needed. Music experiences in Sunday School, Training Union, Woman's Missionary Union, and Brotherhood include participation in group singing and listening worshipfully to music played and sung. Appropriate music for these occasions will be supplied by the

Music Ministry working in cooperation with organizational leaders. Competent music personnel such as song leaders, accompanists, instrumentalists, vocal soloists, and others who will relate properly to the leadership of the respective organizations are always needed. The Music Ministry is responsible for training and supplying these leaders.

As in congregational services, hymnals, pianos, music supplies and equipment must also be provided for use in the organizations of the church. This is a responsibility of the church as it supports its Music Ministry and provides the necessary resources for carrying on the program. Additionally, departments in the various organizations frequently need recordings, record players, rhythm instruments, autoharps, children's songbooks, handbells, and other items which must be supplied for the educational program of the organizations.

II. Lead Persons to Participate in Hymn Singing

Congregational singing is the heart of the church music program. It is a part of every service of worship in which each member can and should participate. It reflects the enthusiasm of the people for their God, their church, and their program for carrying out the divine commission. It is the tie that binds heart, mind, soul, and voice in expression of adoration to God and Christian love one for the other. It is something to be done by the people, not *for* the people.

1. *Congregational Participation*

Christianity is religion in a major key—jubilant, joyous, victorious, and exultant. It has as its greatest inspiration a risen Saviour, a living Lord, and a returning Prince of peace. It has a song of redemption that shall resound through eternity. Indeed it is the singing religion.

Christians will find opportunity for expressing the joys of the Christian religion in many ways, but one unrestrained means is through singing. Singing is a Christian privilege, not a duty or obligation. It is a means whereby each Christian can, and should, express his personal audible praise, adoration, thanksgiving, testimony, and dedication at every opportunity.

When people gather for worship, the singing of the great hymns and gospel songs of the faith constitute tremendous personal and corporate values in worship participation. Hymns of sound doctrinal content, praiseworthy texts, scriptural truths, and meaningful messages help Christians grow in grace and knowledge and contribute significantly both to worship and the learning processes of the individuals who make up the congregation.

Every person in the church should have adequate opportunity to lift his voice to God in praise and adoration in each service of the church. Such singing attunes his heart to God and brings peace, joy, cleansing, refreshment, and renewed strength for the stress of everyday living. Through participation, the singers experience a unifying influence, express feelings that remove burdens, and receive blessings which come as one worships through song. The Music Ministry of the church must do all possible in creating the proper climate for hymn singing by planning, scheduling, and arranging for maximum participation so as to lead all persons to want to join heartily in hymn singing at every opportunity. Adequate time with opportunity for frequent participation in hymn singing should be a characteristic of service planning.

2. *Organizational Participation*

What has been said concerning hymn singing in the congregational worship services applies likewise to singing in the various departmental services and assemblies. With smaller groups it is possible to do much singing and more teaching through the use of didactic hymns which will result in learning experiences. It is practical to correlate the hymns with the lessons to be studied. Hymn singing relevant to the other content being used can be especially meaningful. Through utilization of the Hymn of the Month plan, as well as through careful planning of the worship activities in the departments, it is possible to make music a meaningful part of the worship and educational experience. A further result of effective singing in the organizations will be evidenced in strengthening the singing of the congregational services as department leaders encourage maximum participation on the part of all persons.

3. *Family Living*

Singing in the home is one of the joyful experiences of life. Family devotional periods bring the parents and children closer to God and generate personal warmth and loving appreciation for one another. When each individual in the family participates in hymn singing and other music experiences during worship, the common experience brings lasting satisfaction. Gathering around the piano or sitting in the family room with open hymnals as the family sings together can be a meaningful and binding experience which will live through the years. The Bible has a companion in the hymnal. Through the reading of God's Word and the singing of hymns, the great truths of Christianity may be planted in the minds and hearts of the family members and bear fruit for generations to come. Through wise choice of hymns and the use of good recordings, radio and television programs, the use of church music materials, and by following the suggestions of the church music director for music to use in family devotionals, each family can gain rich experience. Many children play the piano or band or orchestra instruments. The playing of hymns on these instruments as the others sing along can enrich family life. Singing in the home carries over into one's daily work and life.

4. *Varied Occasions*

Church members experience many opportunities for hymn singing. Not only do they share the experience in regular worship services but many have responsibilities for working with missions of the church, visiting institutions for aged and infirm, assisting with jail services, and working in revivals both in their church and outside. Participation in carol sings, special hymn sings, hymn rehearsals, seasonal programs, song sermons, and other special occasions offers opportunities for meaningful hymn singing. Singing of hymns and other songs during church socials, picnics, recreational activities, and fellowship periods brings joyful experiences. At other times such as weddings, funerals, memorial services, observance of the ordinances, church anniversary services, and occasions which bring the church family together, hymn singing is the common denominator for participation and involvement.

For each occasion there must usually be someone responsible for planning the hymn singing, someone to lead, someone to play; and there must be adequate hymnals or songbooks, supplies or equipment suited to the needs of the occasion. The music leaders of the church will need to make adequate provision for these various types of activities and do all possible to contribute to their success.

III. TEACH MUSIC AND HYMNODY

Music is an art dealing with sound, pleasing combinations of tones, and the processes of producing them. Hymnody is the art and act of singing hymns.

We teach music to bring understanding and proficiency to music participation and performance so that the praise of God may be made more glorious. To teach music is to help persons understand the fundamentals of music which involve rhythm, pitch, melody, music notation, and the structure of music. It further involves the discovery and development of technical skills of performance, how music is written and read, and how to translate it into pleasing sounds and musical expression. By teaching music to members of the church, new understandings and appreciations develop which help remove those things which could inhibit their participation in music of the church.

To teach hymnody is to help persons sing the great Christian hymns contained within our hymnals with understanding and assurance. Hymnody is taught as an art and act of singing hymns. It is a contributing factor to one's worship experience when one knows the hymns and sings with spirit and understanding. Through understanding hymnody, persons participate more readily in the music activities of a church and have a greater appreciation for church music and its meaning in Christian worship and life.

1. *Graded Choirs*

In the various age-group choirs of the church, it is possible to teach both music and hymnody. There are important elements of music and basic hymnody appropriate for learning at each age level. A progressive music curriculum should be used to do this.

In the overall church music curriculum, there must be a progressive movement from one age group to the next, musical growth that is continuous from year to year which broadens into appreciation of music and all it means in the functions of the church. Content for the Music Ministry curriculum is contained in the periodicals provided for the various age groups—*The Church Musician* for the adult choirs and Music Ministry leaders. *The Youth Musician* for youth choirs, *The Junior Musician* for the Junior choirs, *Music for Primaries* for the Primary group, and *The Children's Music Leader* for the leaders of the Beginner, Primary, and Junior music groups. Additionally, category 19 books in the Church Study Course contain numerous texts which will help in the teaching of music and hymnody.

2. *Music and Hymnology Classes*

No music program rises above its leadership and the appreciation and participation of the congregation. If a church is to have a fine music program, it must design classes and teach in order to develop the leaders. Each church must feel continuous responsibility in leadership development if it is to have the type of music program which will grow and increasingly involve an expanding circle of church members year by year. These specialized classes may be conducted in many ways. They can meet as a study course group during a week. They may have one-day-a-week sessions, a-night-a-week session, regular classes at certain seasons of the year, or any one of many different plans. Some churches find it most helpful to use I-MAP, which is the Individual Music Advancement Program of home study.

If a church is to have trained music leaders, it must train

them. Only through specialized music classes can this be done. Likewise, if a church is to have informed people in the area of hymnology, which is the study of hymns, it must offer opportunities for studying the great hymns and their meaning in the Christian life. It must provide specialized opportunities through hymnology courses, classes, special units, and other means whereby people may gain at least a basic understanding of music and hymnody.

Classes in music hymnology, music in worship, music in the Bible, and other learning opportunities should be offered the entire congregation for music advancement. When people begin to understand what music is and its many uses and relationships in the Christian life, they gain a new perspective of its use in church functions and are able to have greater appreciation of music in the life and work of the church.

3. *Instrumental*

As in other areas, music learning opportunities must be provided for those persons who have the potential to become organists, pianists, band and orchestra instrumentalists, and handbell ringers for future service throughout the church. Each organization needs pianists who can help them with their work. These persons must first of all understand music fundamentals and other requirements for church music leadership. They must then be developed in utilizing their performing skills in places of service. Classes in hymn playing, accompanying, piano, organ, instrumental ensemble designed to develop performing skills should be maintained on a year-round basis.

IV. TRAIN PERSONS TO LEAD, SING, AND PLAY MUSIC

Trained persons who can take responsibility for leading music, singing, or playing music are needed in every church. This points up a need for *every* church assuming a responsible role in training its own music personnel to serve in the church.

1. *Training Persons to Lead Singing*

In some churches scores of song leaders are needed every Sunday. In others, only a few. But, to have persons who can lead music is an important need which the music program can meet. If a church is to have persons who can lead music capably, it must develop its potential leaders as well as those presently in service. Through the tasks of the Training Union and through other means, potential leaders may be discovered and channeled into the specialized leadership classes conducted by the Music Ministry. Refresher classes for experienced song leaders should be carried on as well as classes in which there is basic instruction for potential leaders. These classes should be scheduled at a time when persons can come and receive the instruction which will contribute most to their development. Such specialized classes are now being conducted during Training Union as a training activity of the church.

In addition to classes for beginning song leaders, classes maintaining in-service training are particularly valuable. Those who are presently engaged in the various organizations of the church should continue to receive instruction each week in the techniques of leading music and in better utilizing their song-leading skills.

2. *Training Persons to Sing*

Training persons to sing music may be done in graded choir, specialized classes, or in general classes, depending on the group to be taught. The graded choir program is one area in which singing techniques and skills may be developed to a fine degree. There may also be graded classes for advanced choir singers, for those who have had some training but need additional training, and for beginners in voice. Private instruction in voice may be offered. Additionally, there may be general classes for members of the congregation who want to gain experience in learning to sing for the enjoyment of it. Thus, specialized classes for all choir singers and general classes for persons who want to learn to sing for enjoyment are a part of the Music Ministry training program.

3. *Training Persons to Play Instruments*

Few churches have more organists and pianists than they need. Consequently, it is desirable to provide regular classes in piano and in organ which offer both potential and present keyboard instrumentalists an opportunity for advancing in their skills and abilities. Classes emphasizing hymn playing, selection of materials, development of techniques, and instruction in basic and advanced repertory provide opportunity for growth. Occasional keyboard seminars and piano festivals afford opportunity for advancing the instrumentalists of the church.

Instruction for those who play band and orchestra instruments and for those who are interested in handbell ringing and the autoharp should be provided. Class instruction, private instruction, and instruction for special needs should be provided on a continuing basis by the Music Ministry.

V. PROVIDE ORGANIZATION AND LEADERSHIP FOR SPECIAL PROJECTS OF THE CHURCH

In this task the Music Ministry joins other church program organizations to supply whatever organization and leadership the church may desire for its projects. Music is closely related to such projects as revival meetings, anniversary celebrations, festivals, seasonal programs, vocal and instrumental recitals, and other special church and community projects.

Revival meetings require revival choir singers, graded choirs, competent instrumentalists, music leaders, and other music resources which will contribute to the music of the revival. Other projects of the church such as anniversary celebrations and special days require music groups, leaders, and resources. Hymn festivals, choir festivals, and hymn playing festivals call for different types of organizations and music leadership. Seasonal programs of the church at Christmas, Easter, Thanksgiving, and during the summer require music organizations, leadership, scheduling, publicizing, and promoting.

With the steadily increasing number of instrumental players in bands and orchestras in schools, colleges, and universities, many churches can have an orchestra or instrumental ensembles which may assist in special projects of the church and will play on stated occasions. Churches having adequate organs may sponsor vesper programs. A recent addition to the music program in many churches is the handbell choir through which the instrumental program finds greater expression.

The relationship of the church to the community in missions projects, carol sings, and the sending of performing groups to hospitals, rest homes, and institutions, provides opportunities for ministering through music and constitutes a means whereby the church can extend its ministry. Also, many churches use radio and television to present the gospel. Such broadcasts and telecasts may draw upon the total music resources of the church to help increase the effectiveness of the church's ministry to the community.

VI. PROVIDE AND INTERPRET INFORMATION REGARDING THE WORK OF THE CHURCH AND THE DENOMINATION

This task is also common with the other church program organizations. With this relationship, the Music Ministry can be used by the church to interpret important information to each of its members. In this way, each member of the Music Ministry can be properly related to the total life and work of the church. It has been found by most ministers of music that church members who are faithful to the various services and activities of the church make the best choir members. Doubtless this is true because these church members are better informed and are, therefore, more devoted to all functions of the church.

Today the organized Music Ministry in Baptist churches is growing rapidly. As a church program organization, it is functioning in approximately half of all Southern Baptist churches. It is realized, however, that music is used in all of the churches whether on an organized basis or not. As churches become aware of how an organized Music Ministry can serve present and future needs through performing its significant tasks, it will increasingly become an organized program in our churches. It is a significant denominational force fully committed to use by the churches and the denomination.

The Church Music Department of the Sunday School Board

is a channel department publishing music periodicals which reach thousands of persons engaged in the music program of the churches. Since music is a part of the total work of the church, its program is related to the other programs. The Music Ministry is a channel of communication for all the programs of the denomination. Hence, those who plan and suggest program materials in the Church Music Department of the Sunday School Board are constantly seeking to use the opportunities they have for channeling other Southern Baptist Convention programs to those engaged in the Music Ministry of the churches.

CHAPTER 9

I. TEACH SYSTEMATIC THEOLOGY, CHRISTIAN ETHICS, CHRISTIAN HISTORY, AND CHURCH POLITY AND ORGANIZATION
  1. Systematic Theology
  2. Christian Ethics
  3. Christian History
  4. Church Polity and Organization

II. GIVE ORIENTATION TO NEW CHURCH MEMBERS

III. TRAIN ALL CHURCH MEMBERS TO WORSHIP, WITNESS, LEARN, AND MINISTER DAILY

IV. TRAIN LEADERS FOR THE CHURCH AND THE DENOMINATION
  1. Discover, Recruit, and Train Potential Leaders
  2. Provide For Specialized Leader Training

V. PROVIDE ORGANIZATION AND LEADERSHIP FOR SPECIAL PROJECTS OF THE CHURCH

VI. PROVIDE AND INTERPRET INFORMATION REGARDING THE WORK OF THE CHURCH AND THE DENOMINATION

9

The Training Program
of a Church

THE TRAINING UNION plays a distinctive role in Southern Baptist churches. It is unique in that it trains all church members and church leaders to accept and perform their full responsibilities. No other denomination has an organization like it. Through their Training Unions, Southern Baptist churches provide training opportunities for members and gain added strength to achieve their tasks.

The Sunday School teaches the biblical revelation. It leads persons to saving faith in Jesus Christ, to membership in a Baptist church, and to growth in the Christian faith and life. Because of these tasks, the Sunday School has an unlimited constituency. It teaches both the saved and the unsaved, the church member and the nonchurch member.

The Training Union, although vitally concerned with evangelism and the growth of Christians, seeks to enrol church members and their children for training. It trains church members to work together within the fellowship of their church and to be effective church members wherever they are. Its primary concern is to train church members to worship, witness, learn, and minister daily. The Training Union succeeds best when all church organizations thrive, when the whole church is strengthened, and when each individual is trained to be a responsible church member.

The Sunday School works with every individual, seeking to lead him to commit his life to Christ and become a useful member of a church. The Training Union works with the individual as a church member—a member of a learning-serving fellowship.

To illustrate this distinction, a track coach may have a brilliant sprinter whose specialty is the one-hundred-yard dash. The coach may develop this athlete to the extent that he wins a number of track events.

In the fall this same sprinter comes out for the football team. The sprinting ability which he developed under the track coach will serve him well as an end on the football team. However, he has many additional tasks to learn as a member of a team. He must learn to master the signals, follow the leadership of his quarterback, catch passes, and do other tasks. All this he must do in cooperation with his teammates. The football coach is no less concerned with him as an individual than is the track coach. He is more concerned, however, with training the athlete to perform as a member of a team.

Anyone who has ever sat through a church business meeting can imagine what it would mean if every church member would learn to play on the same team. If football teams were like some Baptist churches, the ball carrier would be tackled behind his own line by his teammates before he got the ball. A Baptist deacon once said that as long as he was a member of his church it would never have a unanimous vote. This man needs to join the team.

The Sunday School develops persons in the Christian life. The Training Union develops church members to perform as members of the body of Christ. The Sunday School and Training Union differ in purposes as well as in the content of their study programs.

A school of medicine has a specific body of content, and a school of law has a different body of content. Both are schools, yet both may be a part of the same university. This relationship parallels the Sunday School and Training Union.

To understand better the study task of the Training Union, let us consider its content areas, or basic study materials.

I. Teach Systematic Theology, Christian Ethics, Christian History, and Church Polity and Organization

Church members need a growing understanding of several important areas of study if they are to grow in their Christian

faith and serve effectively. They need to grow in their understanding of the great realities of the Christian faith and their
relevance to life today. They need increasing insight into the
ethical implications of the Christian faith and ways to live
daily in the light of the faith they profess. The sweep of Christian history also has much to say about life today. Church
members can profit by studying great movements, moments,
and personalities in Christian history. If church members are
to make their greatest contribution to the kingdom, they need
an ever increasing understanding of ways Christians work together in spreading the gospel.

These broad areas denote the content which is basic to training church members. Study units are developed in terms of
the interests and abilities of persons at various age levels to
become meaningfully involved in these broad areas of membership training. Each of these content areas deserves continuous study.

1. *Systematic Theology*

Theology concerns man's response to God in trust, worship, and understanding. It is man's attempt to understand
who God is, what he does or proposes to do for man, and
what he requires of man. Systematic theology is the attempt
to organize Christian truths into a meaningful system of Christian beliefs according to topics or themes.

Training Union seeks to help persons, through a study of
Christian doctrines, to develop a valid system of Christian
beliefs about God, man, sin and Satan, salvation, the church,
last things, and the Bible.

2. *Christian Ethics*

Christian ethics is the application of the gospel to all of
man's relationships. It involves an exploration of what the
Christian life ought to be in every situation.

Study units in Christian ethics are designed to help persons
grow in Christian principles in every relationship of daily living. These study units include basic principles and norms for
Christian conduct, personal ethics, interpersonal relationships,

relationships of groups, intergroup relationships, family living, Christian citizenship, daily work, and economic life.

3. *Christian History*

Christian history has been defined as "the story of the origin, progress, and development of the Christian religion, and its influence upon the world" (W. J. McGlothlin, *The Course of Christian History*).

Church members can gain much from a study of Christian history. If they see events today in the light of history, they can gain a better understanding of what is happening. Many problems faced now can be dealt with more successfully if one understands how similar situations were dealt with, successfully or unsuccessfully, in the past. A study of great personalities of the past can challenge Christians today. One can better prepare for the future if he has some understanding of trends in Christian history.

Curriculum units in Christian history include studies of great personalities, major issues, significant movements, pivotal events, trends in doctrinal beliefs, and the relationship of the Christian movement to the cultures it has touched.

4. *Church Polity and Organization*

Church polity is the principles of government by which church organization is established and directed. Church organization is the way people are related in a systematic and purposeful arrangement to accomplish objectives. Church organization also includes the way churches organize themselves and function through associations, state conventions, and the Southern Baptist Convention.

A study of church polity and organization helps one to understand principles on which his church organization is based and ways church and denominational organizations function. Such a study helps one better understand ways he can work with others in and through the church in extending the kingdom of God.

Study units cover such areas as the nature, foundations,

scope, and patterns of church polity and organization; the church and its individual members; the church and community life; the church and the state; the church and its work through the association, state convention, Southern Baptist Convention, and the Baptist World Alliance; and the church and interdenominational concerns.

II. Give Orientation to New Church Members

After several years of unprecedented success in winning persons to Christ, Southern Baptists are now being asked, "Where are the converts?" Southern Baptists have led the world in evangelism, but they have not kept all who have been won.

One out of two of those added to church membership rolls is lost to service in and through the church.

Our Sunday School enrolment is the largest in the world; yet it is estimated that only one out of four Southern Baptists attends Sunday School on a given Sunday. No other denomination has the equivalent of the Training Union. Yet in this organization there is a constant shortage of workers. It is estimated that only one out of seven Southern Baptists is in Training Union on a given Sunday.

The ratio of baptisms to church membership is approximately one to thirty. Few of the baptisms result from the witness of lay church members. Pastors and other church staff members do most of the personal witnessing.

More significant in terms of ultimate kingdom progress is the limited commitment of many church members. Many Southern Baptists have a limited concept of Christian discipleship, the church, and church membership as revealed in the New Testament.

Many church members are doing about all they committed themselves to do when they joined the church. Some participate only in the morning worship service because that is all they committed themselves to do when they joined. Many do not witness because they never agreed to witness when they joined the church. Many have not severed questionable social and professional relationships because they never intended to when they came into the church.

Yet these church members are not altogether to blame for the low level of discipleship they demonstrate. The fact is that they have grown up in an easy, undemanding type of religion. Many are not aware of the high demands of the gospel. Many churches do little, beyond a general appeal, to call people to full and meaningful Christian discipleship.

The claims of Christ and the church on the life of one who professes faith in Christ and seeks church membership need to be personalized. Each individual needs to be confronted personally. Both the individual and the church need assurance that the individual has had a genuine conversion. Without a new birth, meaningful involvement in the body of Christ is impossible. Each individual needs a basic understanding of, and a commitment to, the life and the work of the church he seeks to join. Furthermore, each new member needs help at the beginning of his relationship with the church to become vitally and meaningfully involved in its ministry.

Meeting these needs calls for a more careful orientation program than many churches have operated. Giving proper orientation to new church members is a task a church can logically and successfully accomplish through its Training Union. It is a task which requires leadership, organization, materials, and other resources. Detailed plans for accomplishing this task are outlined in the *New Church Member Orientation Manual* by Earl Waldrup.

III. Train All Church Members to Worship, Witness, Learn, and Minister Daily

The New Testament teaches that all church members are to have a part in fulfilling the mission of the church. The need for these members to be trained for effective service grows out of the nature, purpose, and functions of a church. The church is the body of Christ, created to do his work in the world. Every member of the church is to be a functioning part of the body which Christ has created to carry out his will. Each member must develop the capabilities needed, just as a growing child must develop the understandings and skills required to meet the demands of each stage of life.

More than ever before, the gospel must be demonstrated daily in the lives of Christians if it is to be effectively communicated to modern man. Many Christian leaders believe that one of the deepest needs and greatest opportunities of Christian work today is the faithful, day-to-day worship, witness, learning, and ministry by each church member as he goes about his daily activities.

The willingness of church members to become involved in training to improve their ability to worship, witness, learn, and minister daily depends heavily on their understanding of church membership. One who has a scriptural concept of church membership will know that his commitment in joining a church involves an inescapable commitment to function as a part of the body of Christ. Training becomes a natural part of the member's commitment to serve Christ. Every member should be involved in training.

For a new church member, training in becoming a responsible, functioning member begins with new church member orientation. If an effective job is done in developing a scriptural understanding of church membership during orientation, leading the member into additional training will be a natural outcome of his commitment.

Beyond orientation, every church should provide training which enables church members to become increasingly effective as Christian disciples in everyday life. A continuing organization of age-graded departments and unions is essential for offering such training and involving church members in it. Units of study designed to teach systematic theology, Christian ethics, Christian history, and church polity and organization can be offered. Training is provided to improve the ability of church members to perform the functions of their church.

For Juniors through Adults, two organization plans are provided. These make it possible for unions to choose between the regular plan, with its groups and committees, and the alternate plan, with an emphasis on fewer officers, more flexibility, and short-term responsibilities as needed.

Most churches offer continuing church member training on Sunday evening, before or after the worship service. Supplementary sessions of training should be scheduled as needed to meet the needs of all members.

In addition to the church member training just described, churches sometimes find it helpful to offer short-term courses to meet needs of special groups of members or to meet needs directly related to the objectives and goals which the church sets for itself.

The Sunday School Board, in cooperation with other agencies of the Convention, makes available training suggestions and materials to assist churches in carrying on the church member training program. The Christian Training Curriculum provides a comprehensive, balanced coverage of doctrine, Christian ethics, Christian history, and church polity and organization. It also offers training in skills needed for worship, witness, education, and ministry. The Life and Work Curriculum, available after October, 1966, for Young People and Adults, is a fully correlated church curriculum in which the Sunday School, Training Union, Woman's Missionary Union, Brotherhood, and Music Ministry curriculums are related appropriately.

Other materials which offer help for training are *The Baptist Training Union Magazine,* published monthly; resource units; curriculum supplements; Church Study Course books; and the Bible Readers' Course.

It is through the tasks of teaching systematic theology, Christian ethics, Christian history, and church polity and organization, and training all church members to worship, witness, learn, and minister daily that the church training program touches the largest group—church members and their families. Because of this, both ongoing and short-term training deserve attention in planning the work of the church. A church cannot achieve its goals unless adequate training is provided and its members are involved in it.

IV. Train Leaders for the Church and the Denomination

1. *Discover, Recruit, and Train Potential Leaders*

A church's training program should produce leaders for the church. Trained leaders are needed to guide church members to achieve goals they find desirable. The Training Union is the church organization responsible for leading in this task. The definition of the task of training leaders is to "discover, recruit, and train potential leaders for the church and to cooperate with other church organizations in providing specialized training." This task may be seen more clearly when viewed within the context of Training Union's three divisions of training for church members: new church member orientation, church member training, and church leader training. Church leader training consists of potential leader training and specialized leader training.

Potential leader training consists of basic leadership training for potential church leaders. Specialized training consists of specific training for general church officers, leaders of church program organizations, and other organizational units. Church program organizations train their own leaders, with the Training Union assisting them as needed.

Potential leader training is concerned with the discovery, recruitment, and training of those members who show evidence of leadership ability. Potential leaders are discovered in new church member orientation training, church member training, or through contact with leaders and members of the organizational units of the church. Potential leader training consists of training in knowledge, understandings, and skills which are helpful in any area of leadership in the church.

Plans for twenty-six sessions of study and laboratory work are available for potential leader training. Two sessions can be scheduled per week for thirteen weeks. *Training Potential Leaders* is a manual for training leaders. It is designed for use by the leadership training department of the Training Union, and it is available from the Baptist Book Stores. Areas of study include Bible survey; doctrine; Christian discipleship; leadership needs and characteristics; the nature, purpose, and functions of a church; and education and administration principles and methods. Selected books in the Church Study Course are recommended for use in training potential leaders.

2. *Provide for Specialized Leader Training*

One example of specialized training a church should provide is that of vocational guidance. The first major task of the church in vocational guidance is to provide through its educational organizations education in Christian vocations and occupations. The second task is the provision of guidance for occupational choice and adjustment. This involves formal and informal counseling and guidance services to individuals and groups. Nurture and conservation for church vocations volunteers is a third task. The church has an opportunity and obligation to inform its youth about needs and opportunities in church vocations and to create a climate in which God's call to such vocations can be clearly heard.

It is logical for a church to assign the development and promotion of a comprehensive church leader training plan to its Training Union. The general director of the Training Union has responsibility for developing and promoting a comprehensive church leader training plan for the church. In larger churches, the director of church leader training could be given this responsibility. A church leader training unit may be established, with its own leaders, schedules, and curriculum materials. Its leader may be the director of church leader training in the Training Union, or any other qualified person enlisted as an administrative officer of the Training Union in cooperation with the church nominating committee. A leadership training unit may meet on Wednesday nights or at any other time desired.

Specialized leader training provides training for leaders of church program organizations and other organizational units of the church. It usually consists of twenty-six training sessions. Persons enrolled have usually been enlisted for, or express a special interest in, a certain area of work in the program organizations.

The scope of specialized training extends beyond training for service in program organizations. The training of denominational leaders in the association is also a part of specialized training. Training Union also assists in the training of church officers, committee members, and administrative staff groups such as deacons through the use of books in the church administration category of the Church Study Course.

V. PROVIDE ORGANIZATION AND LEADERSHIP FOR SPECIAL PROJECTS OF THE CHURCH

The church training program is ideally equipped to serve the church through providing organization and leadership for special projects of the church. The Training Union is not limited to Sunday evening for the accomplishment of special projects assigned to it by the church.

Many churches have a period of training conducted by the Training Union prior to special revival meetings. The Training Union offers the study of textbooks and resource units showing church members how to witness for Christ. The textbook study is often supplemented with practical experiences in visiting unsaved prospects.

A church may request its Training Union to conduct a training course on stewardship prior to the subscription of the church budget. Through this study each member would be instructed in how to relate the giving of his money to the stewardship of life.

Certain groups may undertake some special studies to deepen their understanding of church membership. These studies may take the form of discussion groups or a study course. One special study project needed by many churches is training members to participate in church business meetings.

The Training Union is the church organization best suited to conduct church projects related to training members to minister to persons of special needs. Also, the Training Union may actually conduct or work with church organizations in conducting many projects relating to ministry as a part of its efforts to train church members in the function of ministry.

The associational Training Union organization annually conducts a one-night training clinic for church officers and committee members. Large churches with trained leaders conduct their own clinics by assigning this responsibility to their Training Unions. These clinics enable churches to begin each year with trained officers and committee members.

These short-term training activities are typical of the special projects a church may assign to its Training Union. Such projects develop specific skills, help a church reach its goals, or involve members in special study and discussion. Training Union leaders should function anywhere, anytime the church has a training need.

VI. PROVIDE AND INTERPRET INFORMATION REGARDING THE WORK OF THE CHURCH AND THE DENOMINATION

The Training Union provides the church with a resource for building a strong and informed church membership. The pastor, the church staff, and the Training Union director should consult with Training Union leaders regarding information which should be interpreted. The significant tasks of the church should be singled out and time given to interpreting them appropriately. In this way the Training Union not only serves as a church educational organization but also becomes a channel for interpreting to its members the life and work of the church.

The church's opportunity of providing and interpreting information to its members through its Training Union is through curriculum materials, activities, and organization and leadership used in the three programs described earlier.

One of the phases of new church member orientation is providing and interpreting information regarding the church and denomination. The degree to which new members become meaningfully involved is related directly to how well they are informed about their church and denomination when they come into the church. Leadership training provides the church a short-term but important opportunity for interpreting the church and denomination to church members.

The graded orientation curriculum provided by the Training Union Department of the Baptist Sunday School Board places a major emphasis on the church and denomination. An age-graded curriculum consisting of both leadership and pupil periodicals for membership training serves as an excellent channel of information regarding the church and denomination. Administration materials and promotional literature provide other channels, as well as resource units, books, and other supplemental materials.

Many activities in the member training program offer opportunities for providing and interpreting information. Planning activities serve to keep leaders informed. Assembly programs, union meetings, study courses, and special projects speak to all church members. Attendance at denominational meetings—associational, state, and Convention-wide—helps members keep informed.

CHAPTER 10

I. PROGRAM SERVICES
   1. Church Library Service
   2. Church Audio-Visual Education Service
   3. Church Recreation Service

II. ADMINISTRATIVE SERVICES
   1. Nominating Committee
   2. Stewardship Committee
   3. Missions Committee
   4. Properties Committee
   5. Personnel Committee

10

The Program Services and the Administrative Services of a Church

IN ADDITION to the program organizations, each church needs certain program services and administrative services. These are significant because of the service they render to individual members, program organizations, and the congregation as a whole. The services which they provide greatly enrich the life and work of the church.

I. PROGRAM SERVICES

The program services of a church are Church Library Service, Church Audio-Visual Education Service, and Church Recreation Service. These services provide resources to church program organizations and, in the case of the library and recreation services, to individual church members. Without these resources the church program organizations would find it difficult to perform fully their tasks. These services properly used inject a vital nutrient into the life and work of the church.

1. *Church Library Service*

In all Baptist churches, there is a continual need for resource materials to aid and supplement the program activities and to help individual members. Individually owned materials are often costly, difficult to obtain, and hard to store for future use. Therefore, it is good stewardship for a church to provide a library service. The church library is a service of providing resource materials to all church programs, program services, administrative services, and personal ministries.

Today's concept of a church library is that of a resource center where all types of resource materials are housed. In this center are printed materials including books, pamphlets, tracts, and clippings. In addition, the library contains audio-visual materials such as slides, filmstrips, maps, recordings, and pictures, and audio-visual equipment and interest-center materials.

These materials are selected to provide tools for training workers, resources for extending the teaching-learning process, and helps for everyday living as the church fulfils its functions of worship, proclamation, education, and ministry.

(1) *Provides resource materials for training workers.*— Thorough training is necessary for all church workers. They must understand how to handle their responsibilities as witnesses to Jesus Christ the Son of God and to serve through his church. To meet the requirements for their tasks, they must study to become approved workmen. They cannot be satisfied with a cursory study of church literature, an incompetent briefing by last year's committee chairman, or impromptu performances. Christ commands that his disciples strive for perfection.

For instance, for adequate preparation, a teacher must know his subject matter thoroughly, understand the group he teaches, and have a working knowledge of appropriate educational methods. While lesson course materials provide regular information, lack of space prohibits thorough treatment in these three areas. The church library then can provide background study aids, Bible commentaries, atlases, dictionaries, and filmstrips to assist the teacher in his study and his teaching. Other resources contain information about age-group psychology and social and educational factors that influence learning. For the Primary teacher who needs to understand the physical, mental, emotional, and social characteristics of the six-year-old, church library materials provide assistance. To learn sound educational methods, the teacher can utilize resources which explain methods and give instructions for preparing and using various types of learning aids.

As teachers must be prepared for their job, so every worker needs to be trained to fulfil his maximum usefulness. The church library is an essential source for materials to assist Sunday School teachers, Training Union leaders, deacons, committee chairmen, and ushers.

(2) *Provides resource materials for extending the teaching-learning process.*—The church library also provides materials for extending the teaching-learning process. Few students would earn a college degree if they limited their study to a quick scan of their texts and the brief periods in their classes. To learn a subject thoroughly, research is necessary, audio-visual aids are needed to give permanence to learning, and participation is essential to make learning personal. This is also true for the people participating in the Sunday School, Training Union, Woman's Missionary Union, Brotherhood, Music Ministry programs, and other learning activities. Each person must assume the responsibility for individual study and preparation.

Extending the learning process requires resources. Many people cannot provide the books they need; fewer still can personally furnish audio-visual materials for a teaching-learning situation. However, an efficiently operating church library can make available these materials. In fact, the staff is alert to content areas in the organizations and has ready when the study groups need them the materials recommended in church literature and in Church Study Course books.

For instance, when Adults are studying a particular unit on communism, the library provides books, flip charts, and films to help union members make a thorough and extensive study. So with every learning situation—the preaching period, Sunday School, missions study, music activities—the church library is a partner by relating materials to the subjects studied and by encouraging their use.

(3) *Provides resource materials for meeting needs in everyday living.*—In addition to providing tools for training workers, and resources for extending the teaching-learning process, the

church library has a major responsibility of supplying helps for meeting needs in everyday living.

While the pastor, deacons, and other church members want to minister to the individual needs of people in the church, they cannot meet all the needs. However, resources from the church library can frequently go where visitors cannot go. At other times, they can go with the visitor and remain long after he has left. Often they meet the needs known only to the individual when no visitor is involved. Resources can provide counsel in family living, solace in bereavement, comfort in illness, guidance in vocations, assurance in times of doubt, and strength in temptation.

As the church fulfils its functions of worship, proclamation, education, and ministry, the church library provides resources essential to train workers, educate the people, and minister to the congregation and the community. To reach this objective, the church library selects discriminately, processes accurately, circulates systematically.

(4) *Provides for care and circulation of resource materials.*—The library, through a systematic process, cares for materials in order to obtain fullest value from each item purchased. The library staff prepares material for use and repairs items damaged in use. Audio-visual materials and equipment require careful maintenance, for they must be kept in satisfactory operating condition if they are to be of value.

In preparing materials, the staff classifies them so that they may be arranged in a logical order. The card catalog is essential in caring adequately for materials. Maintaining an up-to-date catalog insures that borrowers may know about and locate materials.

Along with caring for materials, the church library circulates them by a systematic method. Specifically designated library hours are scheduled, publicized, and maintained. These hours are determined by the needs of the church members. A member of the library staff is on duty at each of the designated times. The staff members assist borrowers in finding materials and by making suggestions or recommendations when appropriate.

2. *Church Audio-Visual Education Service*

The present generation of Baptists is the first to enjoy the benefits of audio-visuals. The identification of all films with Hollywood led Baptist churches to reject the use of audio-visuals for many years. More recently, however, congregations have realized that audio-visuals can motivate persons in decision-making.

Since Christianity is primarily a life of decision-making for God, this new discovery has real significance. Churches can strengthen their challenge to Christlike living through the appropriate use of audio-visuals.

Audio-visuals can also improve learning. Churches have discovered that audio-visuals can assist persons to learn more rapidly, to learn better, and to learn more. Because audio-visuals serve all the programs of the church, the congregation should assign the following responsibilities.

(1) *Program the use of audio-visuals.*—Many Baptist churches now own audio-visual equipment, films, and filmstrips and enjoy the results that come from their use. In churches where audio-visual materials are available, many leaders have not learned how to use them to improve their work. A church is obligated to plan with its leaders the use of audio-visuals to enrich their work. This is the beginning place for an audio-visual education service.

Many churches believe that the purchase of a piece of equipment or of a particular filmstrip is all that is needed. But only when equipment and materials are being used in learning situations does the church see these investments pay. A church should elect a director of audio-visual education service (DAVE) and assign to him the responsibility for leading the church's workers to understand the value of these resources and to use them.

Many films and filmstrips have been produced in recent years. Some are of value in assisting teachers in their task of instruction. Others have been prepared to dramatize life situations and to challenge persons to commit themselves to the work of Christ. Few church leaders are acquainted with the vast amount of material available. DAVE makes his contribution here by knowing what is available, recommending its purchase or rental, and recommending its use to specific workers for specific purposes and dates. In large churches he should be assisted by an elected audio-visual education consultant assigned to serve each educational organization.

(2) *Train equipment operators to assist leaders.*—One of the major handicaps to more extensive and better use of audio-visuals is the lack of skill in operating motion-picture and filmstrip projectors. A real service is rendered by equipment operators who have been thoroughly trained to handle all details of a film or filmstrip projection. This means convenience for audio-visual users and economy for the church through proper care and maximum use of equipment.

Leaders themselves need to be trained in the basic principles of audio-visual education. This includes the biblical basis of audio-visual education, what audio-visuals can do, and the elements of an effective audio-visual presentation. But service-minded church audio-visual education service personnel can and should relieve the individual church leader of having to obtain materials and set up and operate equipment. It should be as easy for workers to use audio-visuals as any other medium of communication. An adequately staffed and properly functioning church audio-visual education service is the surest way to make this possible.

3. *Church Recreation Service*

Jesus made it clear in his brief earthly ministry that he was interested in every aspect of the individual's total life and personality.

Whether the problem was physical, mental, or spiritual, he met the individual's particular need. He healed the blind and lame, dismissed demons, forgave the sin tortured, met the social needs of those he sought to influence, and drew his followers aside for renewal in quiet places.

Churches today must show a like concern. The use of recreation as a medium in this complete ministry is not only appropriate but necessary.

Recreation is not purely physical or social, but, according to the situation, it may encompass all wholesome activity. Recreation is useful in virtually every phase of religious education. Through its unique processes lives can be touched and changed.

The purpose of church recreation is basically the same as that of all church activity: to lead the lost to Christ, and to develop those within the Christian fellowship toward Christ-likeness.

Times have changed since the early days of the church, and they will, of course, continue to change. Today in an ever increasing measure, the wise use of recreation is essential to meeting the opportunities afforded our churches.

A large percentage of the millions of Southern Baptist adults live in the city and work inside. Their only exercise during the day is walking within a building or on their way to and from lunch. When they arrive home in the evening, it is too dark for them to spend much time outdoors. Under such conditions it is no wonder that emotional tension is a characteristic of our age. As our society becomes more urbanized, churches must give more consideration to a ministry in which church members may release their pent-up emotions in a healthy manner.

Social graces and habits are harmonious with Christian teachings. More and more in our society the individual is being overlooked. Common courtesies of a few years ago are almost ignored today. Surely churches, along with families, have the responsibility to develop in their members those graces which will make them attractive to the world.

Beauty is of God. The highest experiences a man can have are always closely related to his idea of beauty. Church recreation should provide means by which individual persons can become beautiful in their actions, habits, and expressions.

Recreation not only helps build strong bodies and gives new avenues of expression but also provides another means of Christian fellowship. As churches grow in size and as time schedules become more exacting, church members spend less time in relaxed fellowship with one another. They hurry to church, sit in classes or unions, hurry to worship services, and they hurry home. Congregations need opportunities when they can come together in relaxed fellowship. Out of such experiences friendships develop. Such friendships are vital to the ongoing mission of a church.

In meeting these needs and making the most of these opportunities, the church will include every age group and provide for as wide a variety of needs as possible. The most active participants should not dictate the total direction of the program. Often the least active individual has the greatest need. For example, the growing host of older adults need attention, although they will not overly demand such consideration.

Not only the more common social and physical activities should be utilized, but creative activities such as drama, arts, and crafts offer additional opportunities. Camping and outing activities are important. Music and cultural opportunities are a part of all effective programs. Though often used in connection with a given program emphasis, service activities offer wonderful possibilities for recreative use of time.

An effective church recreation committee is the agent by which a church can assure the proper use of its recreation opportunities.

The work of this committee generally falls into five categories.

(1) *Discover the recreation interests and capabilities of the membership.*—The committee should survey the church membership to find out what their leisure time interests are and what recreation leadership potential there is within the church family. The survey should be worked out in cooperation with the Sunday School leaders and the church council. This survey will serve to acquaint the committee with the church's interests, and the survey should be designed to give the committee the actual names of potential recreation leaders.

(2) *Coordinate the total recreation program of the church.*—The chairman of the committee will work with the church council or similar planning body to help coordinate the recreation activities carried on by the various organizations

and the committee itself. For example, the committee should avoid scheduling a basketball game on the same night as a valentine banquet. The committee will also try to suggest activities that will provide balance. To do this the chairman should keep up-to-date records of all the activities for which his committee is responsible. He should also seek to know as much as possible about the recreation plans of the various church organizations.

As an ex officio member of the church council, he should serve the council in the recreation area and bring items of importance to them as need arises. The council should call on the recreation committee when needs in the recreation ministry are discovered.

(3) *Assist in training and providing resources for leaders charged with the responsibility for recreation activities in their respective organizations.*—Whenever possible, this training should be provided in conjunction with the church's Training Union organization.

For example, since the associate superintendents of all Sunday School departments are responsible for the social and fellowship activities of their departments, the recreation committee should see that special social recreation training is offered to these officers early in the church year.

(4) *Assist organizational leaders with specific recreation projects.*—The recreation committee should be prepared to assist the leaders of the church organizations when they need help with some specific activity. These requests may take numerous forms. Perhaps a Junior leader may need a new idea for a party for her group; an Intermediate worker may need help in planning an overnight retreat or preparing a lakeside service for that retreat; or the Woman's Missionary Society may need assistance in staging a coronation or directing a special dramatic presentation.

(5) *Plan, promote, and direct recreation activities not directly sponsored by a specific organization.*—Some recreation activities of the church will not be sponsored by or through any particular church organization. The sports program, for instance, should be promoted through the organizations but

will generally be directed by the recreation committee working with the local leagues. The church also may ask the recreation committee to take the responsibility for the summer camp or day-camp activities.

Every congregation should determine how recreation can contribute to the church's basic functions of worship, proclamation, education, and ministry. This question can be answered by a church after it is fully informed about the values of the recreation service. As in the other church programs, objectives should be clearly stated to show the place of recreation in the total church program. When these considerations are settled and priorities established, sufficient leadership, finances, and facilities of the church should be allocated to meet these needs.

II. ADMINISTRATIVE SERVICES

Each church must provide leadership, finances, facilities, and administrative controls to serve the programs it establishes. These items are necessary elements in the continuing operation of each program. Though the church must provide these, it is difficult for the church as a whole to plan, coordinate, and evaluate their procurement and administration. The church, therefore, elects certain groups of its members to represent the whole church. These groups working together become organizations usually called church committees.

Church committees can be classified into two types— regular, or standing committees, and special committees. Regular committees have a continuing job to perform for the church. Though their job responsibilities should be evaluated and updated periodically, their responsibility relates to the church's ongoing work. Special committees perform a temporary service for the church. When their job is completed, the committees are discontinued. Both types of committees provide an essential service for the church.

Each church must decide what administrative services it needs. It must also determine and assign responsibility to each committee. The following list suggests some of the regular committees and their responsibility.

1. *Nominating Committee*

Principal Function: The purpose of the church nominating committee is to coordinate the staffing of church-elected leadership positions to be filled by volunteers.

RESPONSIBILITIES:

1. Select, interview, and enlist the church program organization leaders, church committee chairmen, and general church officers
2. Approve prospective workers prior to contact by church leaders
3. Distribute church leadership according to priority needs
4. Assist church leaders to discover and enlist qualified personnel to fill and maintain church-elected positions
5. Recommend volunteer leaders to the church for election
6. Recommend persons to serve on special committees as the church directs

2. *Stewardship Committee*

Principal Function: The stewardship committee develops and recommends an overall stewardship information plan and administers the gifts of church members, using sound principles of financial management.

RESPONSIBILITIES:

1. Promote stewardship throughout the year
2. Plan the annual church budget
3. Conduct the church budget subscription
4. Administer the church budget

3. *Missions Committee*

Principal Function: The principal function of the missions committee is to discover possibilities for local mission projects, share findings with church program organizations, and serve the church in establishing and conducting such mission projects as may be assigned to it.

RESPONSIBILITIES:

1. Survey and analyze possibilities for local mission projects that can be sponsored by the church
2. Work with the church council as it coordinates the work of the missions committee with the mission activities of program organizations. When requested, the committee works with the church program organizations in providing them assistance in the mission work they do for the church
3. Work with church stewardship committee and/or budget committee in accordance with church procedures to secure any needed financial support of mission projects
4. Procure facilities, prescribe operating procedures, and operate mission projects assigned to it by the church
5. Accept appropriate responsibility for starting new churches in proper relationship to church program organizations
6. Communicate with the associational missions committee, as needed, concerning mission needs in the association. It interprets these needs to the church and responds as authorized by the church

4. *Properties Committee*

Principal Function: The properties committee assists a church in matters related to properties administration. Its work includes such areas as maintaining all church properties for ready use; recommending policies regarding use of properties; recommending employment of maintenance personnel; and assigning responsibilities to personnel for supervision.

RESPONSIBILITIES:

1. Inspect and inventory church properties
2. Recommend employment, training, and supervision of maintenance personnel
3. Develop and initiate scheduled cleaning procedures for church facilities
4. Develop and recommend program of preventive maintenance
5. Develop and recommend policies for use of church facilities and equipment
6. Request and administer maintenance, furniture, and equipment budget

5. *Personnel Committee*

Principal Function: The principal function of the personnel committee is to study and advise the church in matters relating to the employed staff.

RESPONSIBILITIES:

1. Study and evaluate the employed staff needs of the church
2. Recommend the creation of employed positions to meet the church's needs
3. Prepare and recommend employed staff policies to the church, such as job descriptions, salary, staff benefits
4. Recruit, interview, and recommend new staff members to the church

The preceding list is by no means exhaustive of what many churches feel their administrative service needs require. However, these comprise some of the more essential regular committees in most churches. Other regular committees might include a public relations committee, a nursery committee, a kitchen committee, a church history committee, an insurance committee, a flower committee, a baptism committee, a Lord's Supper committee, and a benevolence committee. Churches should be careful to establish only those administrative service committees they need. There are two principles in this regard which are especially important: (1) Committee work should be determined on the basis of need; and (2) The number of committees should be determined on the basis of well-defined areas of work.

SUGGESTIONS FOR THE TEACHER

CHAPTERS 1 AND 2

A teacher may approach the first two chapters with a similar method. Place the outline of each chapter on the chalkboard. Ask the class members to search their Bibles, using the concordance, to locate verses or passages of Scripture which contribute to the understanding of the outlines. If the class is large, it may be divided into subgroups and assigned a section of the outline to develop. Use findings to enlarge, correct, or give added understanding to what the authors have written.

CHAPTER 3

Select a business (farming or homemaking may be seen as such) understood by the class. Get their help in analyzing the kinds of activities common to the business. List activities. Group activities according to their most common purpose. Discuss how these may be assigned for carrying out. Draw parallel to work of church as expressed in chapter 2.

CHAPTER 4

Use church covenant, constitution, and bylaws to show how the church has expressed itself as to objectives and operational policies. Show how previous minutes of church business meetings record actions taken by congregation and those delegated to pastor, staff, or deacons.

Teacher could allow class members to write down any group responsibilities which they feel he should have. Let group indicate who may assist pastor with various responsibilities.

CHAPTERS 5-9

If available, ask church program organization leaders to serve as resource panel for these chapters. Ask each to present a brief statement of tasks assigned to his program. Illustrate how the organizations could cooperate, according to tasks, on a common goal or project, such as a missions action project, the Church Growth Plan, or the special missions offerings.

Teacher should discuss in detail the chapters showing that the content is concerned with work to be done. Lead the class to review and evaluate in each case whether the task is being done and how well.

CHAPTER 10

If the church does not have services, a field trip to a church which does might be taken. Discussion of immediate needs being met and not being met by these services could be reviewed. Have the class evaluate the facilities now available for each service and discuss the adequacy of each. Discuss the concept of the program organizations and the service organizations. After discussing the work of each, list ways the service could be improved.

FOR REVIEW AND WRITTEN WORK

CHAPTER 1

1. What is an organism?
2. What words best describe the true nature of a church?
3. What are the "parts" of the body of Christ?
4. How does a church get its unity?

CHAPTER 2

5. List three Scripture references which give clues to the purpose of a church.
6. Define in your own words the purpose of a church.
7. What is meant by "a function of a church"?
8. Name the four functions of a church.

CHAPTER 3

9. What is the beginning point in organizing a church?
10. Name three types of tasks a church may have.
11. What is programing?
12. How many aspects form the framework for programing?
13. State the five principles of programing.

CHAPTER 4

14. Name six responsibilities of the congregation.
15. Why should a church set objectives?
16. Describe how a pastor ministers through administration.

CHAPTER 5

17. What is meant by the "biblical revelation"? What does it contain?
18. Why is the task of leading in reaching all prospects assigned to the Sunday School?
19. Name the four functions of the church, and give an example of the way the Sunday School may lead members to perform each one.
20. How does your Sunday School help the church in special projects? Give at least three examples.

CHAPTER 6

21. List the tasks of Woman's Missionary Union.
22. Discuss the scope of the content area of missions. Why is teaching missions important for a church?

23. Discuss the relationship of study and other actions in Woman's Missionary Union. List the areas in which WMU leads persons to participate in missions.

24. What is the relationship of missions projects to the ongoing program of WMU?

Chapter 7

25. What are the four tasks a church normally expects a Brotherhood program to do?

26. Name the four major areas which make up the missions teaching task for men, young men, and boys.

27. Name three general ways men, young men, and boys can participate in missions activities.

28. List four special projects of the church which need the help of all of the organizations, including Brotherhood.

Chapter 8

29. Name the six tasks of the Music Ministry and give a brief interpretation of each.

30. How would you establish a music training program in your church and what training would you offer?

31. How can graded choirs contribute to music growth in your church?

Chapter 9

32. Explain the distinction between the Sunday School and the Training Union. What is the primary concern of each organization?

33. List the four broad content or study areas of Training Union.

34. Write in your own words why you believe a Baptist church needs to provide effective new member orientation.

35. Explain the difference between potential leader training and specialized leader training.

36. List the six tasks of Training Union. Check those tasks (if any) *not* being done by the Training Union in your church.

Chapter 10

37. What are the purposes of the library service?

38. How can churches improve their work by using audio-visuals?

39. Discuss briefly the spiritual ministry of a church through the recreation service.

40. Discuss briefly why a church needs committees.

GLOSSARY

Administration—The process of leading people as a group to achieve common goals.

Administrative controls—The means for exercising control, such as policies, procedures, objectives, duties.

Administrative service—One or more basic continuing actions of administration grouped together to serve the congregation and its leaders.

Areas of work—Statements of intention to achieve balanced results from work within the range of a church's function.

Biblical foundations—A statement of biblical teachings believed to be foundational to a church's programing and planning.

Channel organization—A Southern Baptist Convention organization which not only discovers, develops, and interprets its own program but also interprets through its materials and programs the work of other Southern Baptist Convention agencies.

Content area—The material selected for presentation on a specific subject basic to the church function of education.

Educate—The process of leading persons to the knowledge and acceptance of Jesus Christ as Saviour and Lord, of teaching and training the church's constituency to perform the functions of their church, and of helping them develop toward full Christian maturity.

Educational organization—An organization having clearly defined constituency and content areas properly related to those of other church organizations, and offering a structured approach to learning growing out of a church's philosophy and objectives, and consisting of program learning activities conducted by organizational leaders.

Finances—The monetary resources required to carry on the church's program.

Function—A basic kind of action which is consistent with the nature of a church.

Goals—Statements of intention to accomplish a measurable quantity and/or quality of results by a specific time.

Leaders-Members—Power available from, or supplied by, the physical and mental efforts of church members.

164

Minister—The act of making a loving response to the needs of persons in Jesus' name.

Need—An urgent necessity either within or outside which a church must inevitably and unavoidably face.

Opportunity—A need in the context of a favorable set of circumstances.

Objectives—Statements of a church's intention.

Organism—A living being or thing composed of functioning parts but with the element of life being independent of, and more fundamental than, the parts making up the whole.

Organization—An orderly arrangement of leaders and members, in relationship to one another, according to their assigned responsibilities in carrying out the program of a church.

Organized—A state of being completely whole as a result of the arrangement of related parts.

Overarching objective—A statement of timeless intention to act in accordance with an unchanging purpose.

Philosophy—A statement of concepts which serves as a guide in conducting a church's programs.

Policy—The settled course adopted and followed by an institution or body.

Program services—One or more basic continuing activities grouped together for performance in support of programs.

Program plan—An established and approved group of tasks, identified as a program, program service, or administrative service, which form a base for planning detailed activities.

Program—One or more basic continuing activities of primary importance grouped together for performance in moving a church toward its objectives.

Proclaim—The act of declaring what God has done in and through Jesus Christ for the salvation of men.

Purpose—God's timeless, unchanging intention for a church.

Strategy—A natural pattern of essential actions used in achieving a goal.

Task—A basic continuing activity, the performance of which is necessary to assist a church in achieving its purpose.

Relationships—A statement which includes *what* relates groups, *how* they relate, and *when* they relate.

Worship—The act of experiencing an awareness of God, of adoring him in recognition of his holiness and majesty, and of responding in loving obedience to his leadership.